Excel® 2016 The

30 Most Common
Formulas & Features
The Step-By-Step Guide

C.J. Benton

Thank you!

Thank you for purchasing and reading this book! **<u>Your feedback is valued and appreciated</u>**. Please take a few minutes and leave a review.

Other Books Available From This Author:

1. Microsoft® Excel® Start Here The Beginners Guide

2. The Step-By-Step Guide To The **25 Most Common** Microsoft® Excel® Formulas & Features *(version 2013)*

3. The Step-By-Step Guide To **Pivot Tables &** Introduction To **Dashboards** *(version 2013)*

4. **Excel® Pivot Tables & Introduction To Dashboards** The Step-By-Step Guide *(version 2016)*

5. The Step-By-Step Guide To The **VLOOKUP** formula in Microsoft® Excel®

6. The Microsoft® Excel® Step-By-Step Training Guide **Book Bundle**

7. **Excel® Macros & VBA For Business Users** - A Beginners Guide

8. **Microsoft® Word® Essentials** The Step-By-Step Guide

Table of Contents

CHAPTER 1
How To Use This Book

This book can be used as a tutorial or quick reference guide. It is intended for users who are just getting started with the fundamentals of Microsoft® Excel®, as well as for users who understand the basics and now want to build upon this skill by learning the more common intermediate level Excel® formulas and features.

While this book is intended for beginners, it does assume you already know how to create, open, save, and modify an Excel® workbook and have a general familiarity with the Excel® Ribbon (toolbar).

All of the examples in this book use **Microsoft® Excel® 2016**, however most of the functionality and formulas can be applied with Microsoft® Excel® version 2013. All screenshots use **Microsoft® Excel® 2016,** functionality and display will be slightly different if using **Excel® 2013.**

Please always **back-up your work** and **save often**. A good best practice when attempting any new functionality is to **create a copy of the original spreadsheet** and implement your changes on the copied spreadsheet. Should anything go wrong, you then have the original spreadsheet to fall back on. Please see the diagram below.

Diagram 1:

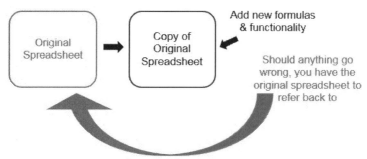

This book was written in the United States, therefore many of the exercises use the US dollar currency symbol **$**. For instructions on how to change the currency symbol, for example to the **British Pound £** or **Euro €**, please see 'Currency Formatting', page 105.

This book is structured into five sections. Part one focuses on basic formulas. This is where users who are just beginning to learn Excel® would typically start. The next three segments are intended for intermediate level users, they examine the features of Pivot Tables, Data Validation, Conditional Formatting, and supporting Text Functions that may be used when troubleshooting Pivot Table reports and other common formula errors. Concluding with part five, which introduces the advanced Excel® functionality of the VLOOKUP, AND, & IF functions.

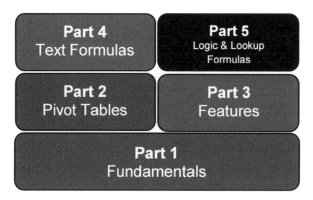

The table below is a summary of the functionality and features detailed in each part:

PART 1 – Formula Fundamentals	
Chapters 2 - 6 13 Functions	• Addition (Sum), Subtraction, Multiplication, & Division • Average, Minimum, & Maximum • Today & Networkdays • SumIF, CountIF, CountIFS, & AverageIF
PART 2 - Introduction To Pivot Tables	
Chapter 7 1 Feature	• How to create a basic Pivot Table • Formatting Pivot Table results • Adding additional rows (categories) to your report • Inserting Pivot Charts
PART 3 – Excel® Features	
Chapters 8 - 12 6 Features	• Data Sorting • Filtering (AutoFilter) • Formula Trace • Text-To-Columns • Conditional Formatting • Data Validation
PART 4 – Text Functions	
Chapters 13 - 14 7 Functions	• LEN & TRIM • PROPER, UPPER, & LOWER • CONCAT & MID
PART 5 – Logic & Lookup Formulas	
Chapters 15 & 16 3 Functions	• IF & AND *(formulas)* • VLOOKUP *(basics)*

FILES FOR EXERCISES

The exercise files used in this book are available for download at the following website:
http://bentonexcelbooks.my-free.website/excel-2016

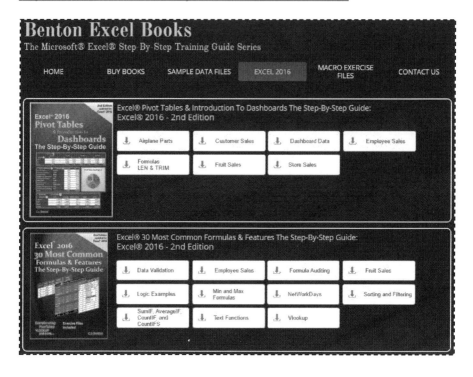

CHAPTER 2

Basic Formulas

Below are the fundamental formulas most beginners learn first.

ARITHMETIC APPLICATION	OPERATOR	DEFINITION
Sum (Addition)	+	Adds two or more cells or numbers together
Subtraction	-	Subtracts two or more cells or numbers
Multiplication	*	Multiplies two or more cells or numbers
Division	/	Divides two or more cells or numbers

Step-By-Step Examples:

SUM (Addition)

1. Begin by creating a new blank Excel® spreadsheet, from your keyboard press shortcut keys **(CTRL+N)** or click the **'New Document'** icon from the **'Quick Access'** toolbar:

2. Enter the following numbers into **column 'A'**
   a. Cell **'A1'** enter the number **2**
   b. Cell **'A2'** enter the number **3**
   c. Cell **'A3'** enter the number **1**
   d. Cell **'A4'** enter the number **2**

The spreadsheet should look similar to the following:

	A
1	2
2	3
3	1
4	2
5	

3. Click cell **'A5'**

4. From the Ribbon select the tab **'Formulas'**

5. Click the ∑ **AutoSum** drop-down box

6. Press the **'Enter'** button on your keyboard

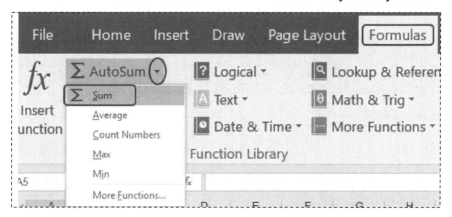

The result should be **8**:

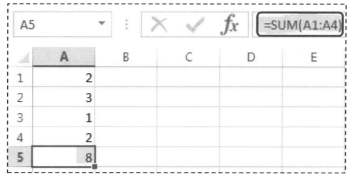

Alternatively, you may also **type the following into cell 'A5'**:

1. Enter the **equal =** symbol from your keyboard

2. Type **sum(**

3. Select (highlight) rows **'A1:A4'**

4. Press the **'Enter'** button on your keyboard

SUBTRACTION

Using the same the sample data as the 'Sum' section:

1. Start by clicking cell **'B3'**

2. Enter the **equal =** symbol from your keyboard

3. Click cell '**A2**'

4. Enter the **minus -** symbol from your keyboard

5. Click cell '**A3**'

6. Press the '**Enter**' button on your keyboard

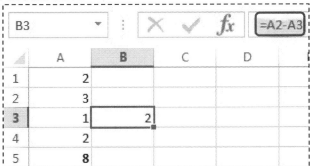

The result should be **2**:

MULTIPLICATION

Using the same the sample data as the 'Sum' section:

1. Start by clicking cell **'B4'**

2. Enter the **equal =** 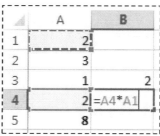 symbol from your keyboard

3. Click cell '**A4**'

4. Enter the **asterisk *** symbol from your keyboard

5. Click cell '**A1**'

6. Press the '**Enter**' button on your keyboard

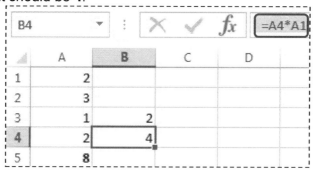

The result should be **4**:

DIVISION

Using the same the sample data as the 'Sum' section:

1. Start by clicking cell '**C4**'

2. Enter the **equal =** symbol from your keyboard

3. Click cell '**B4**'

4. Enter the **forward slash /** symbol from your keyboard

5. Click cell '**B3**'

6. Press the '**Enter**' 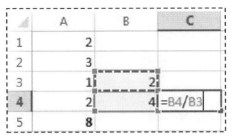 button on your keyboard

The result should be **2**:

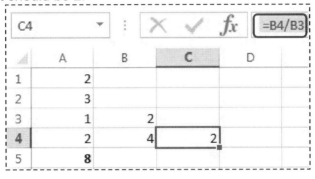

CHAPTER 3

Calculating Averages

FUNCTION	DEFINITION
Average	Returns the average number in a range of values, does not include text in the evaluation

Quick Example:

Syntax:

```
AVERAGE(number1, [number2], ...)
Number1 is required, subsequent numbers are optional
```

| A4 | | | ▼ | ⋮ | ✕ ✓ *fx* | =AVERAGE(A2:A3) |

	A	B	C	D	E
1	**SALES**				
2	$100				
3	$200				
4	$150				

Step-By-Step Example:

Average Function

1. Begin by creating a new Excel® spreadsheet
2. Enter the following numbers into **column 'A'**
   a. Cell '**A1**' enter the label '**SALES**'
   b. Cell '**A2**' enter the number **$100**
   c. Cell '**A3**' enter the number **$200**
   d. Cell '**A4**' enter the number **$300**
   e. Cell '**A5**' enter the number **$400**

The spreadsheet should look similar to the following:

	A
1	**SALES**
2	$100
3	$200
4	$300
5	$400

3. Click cell **'A6'**

4. From the Ribbon select the **'Formulas'** tab

5. Click the ∑ **AutoSum** drop-down box

6. Select **'Average'**

7. Press the **'Enter'** button on your keyboard

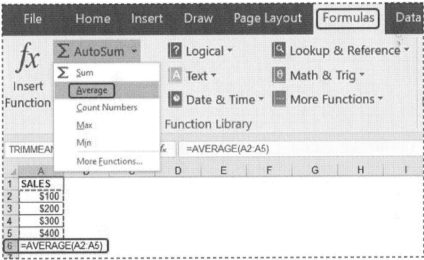

The result should be an average of **$250**:

Alternatively, you may also enter the following into cell '**A6**':

1. Enter the **equal =** ⊞ symbol from your keyboard
2. Type **average(**
3. Select (highlight) rows '**A2:A5**'

4. Press the '**Enter**' ⊞ button on your keyboard

CHAPTER 4

Determining the Minimum & Maximum number in a list

FUNCTION	DEFINITION
MIN	Returns the lowest number in a range of values, does not include text in the evaluation
MAX	Returns the largest number in a range of values, does not include text in the evaluation

Quick Examples: MIN & MAX

Syntax:
MIN(number1, [number2], ...)
Number1 is required, subsequent numbers are optional

B2		⋮	✕	✓	*fx*	=MIN(A2:A4)

	A	B	C	D	E
1	LIST	MIN	MAX		
2	1	1			
3	2				
4	3				

MAX(number1, [number2], ...)
Number1 is required, subsequent numbers are optional

C2		⋮	✕	✓	*fx*	=MAX(A2:A4)

	A	B	C	D	E
1	LIST	MIN	MAX		
2	1	1	3		
3	2				
4	3				

WEB ADDRESS & FILE NAME FOR EXERCISE:
http://bentonexcelbooks.my-free.website/excel-2016
MinAndMaxFormulas.xlsx

Step-By-Step Example:

Sample data, due to space limitations **the entire data set is not displayed**.

	A	B	C	D	E	F	G
	SALES PERSON FIRST NAME	SALES PERSON LAST NAME	QUARTER	TOTAL		BEST SALES	WORST SALES
1							
2	Jack	Smith	1	$ 343			
3	Jack	Smith	2	$ 1,849			
4	Jack	Smith	3	$ 2,653			
5	Jack	Smith	4	$ 5,494			
6	Joe	Tanner	1	$ 377			
7	Joe	Tanner	2	$ 2,404			
8	Joe	Tanner	3	$ 3,980			
9	Joe	Tanner	4	$ 39,631			
25	Billy	Winchester	4	$ 8,516			

Max

1. Open the spreadsheet MinAndMaxFormulas.xlsx

2. Place your cursor in cell **'F2'**

3. From the Ribbon select the **'Formulas'** tab

4. Click the ∑ **AutoSum** drop-down box

5. Select **'Max'**

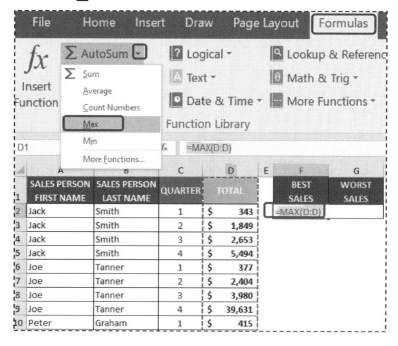

6. Select **column 'D'**

7. Press the **'Enter'** button on your keyboard

Min

1. Open the MinAndMaxFormulas.xlsx spreadsheet

2. Place your cursor in cell **'G2'**

3. From the Ribbon select the **'Formulas'** tab

4. Click the ∑ **AutoSum** drop-down box

5. Select **'Min'**

6. Select **column 'D'**

7. Press the **'Enter'** button on your keyboard

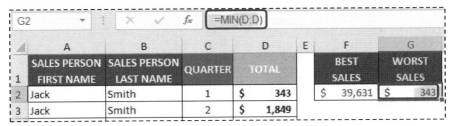

The results should be:
```
39,631 Best Sales Results
   343 Worst Sales Results
```

Alternatively, you may also enter the following into cell '**F2**':

1. Enter the **equal =** symbol from your keyboard

2. Type **max(**

3. Select column '**D**'

4. Press the '**Enter**' button on your keyboard

or for **MIN**:

You may enter the following into cell '**G2**':

1. Enter the **equal =** symbol from your keyboard

2. Type **min(**

3. Select column '**D**'

4. Press the '**Enter**' key on your keyboard

☑ Additional Information:

All the functions reviewed in chapters 2 – 4 may also be accomplished using Pivot Tables, which are introduced in chapter 7. However, sometimes it is faster to use one of the above formulas when your sample size is small or you're simply providing these results in an email, IM (instant message), or text.

Similarly, these are very useful functions when you want to quickly double check your Pivot Table results. It's always worthwhile to validate your results to ensure you're not missing any values. By taking just a few extra minutes to verify your calculations, you'll likely catch any mistakes, improve your creditability with customers, and have the confidence to defend your work should it ever be questioned.

CHAPTER 5

Basic Date & Time Functions

FUNCTION	DEFINITION
TODAY	Provides today's date. *NOTE: this formula will update each day, it is always the current date*
NOW	Provides today's date and time. *NOTE: this formula will update each day, it is always the current date*
NETWORKDAYS	Calculates the number of **workdays (Monday – Friday)** between two dates

Quick Examples:

TODAY & NOW (functions)

There are no parameters for the **'Today()'** or **'Now()'** functions.

	A	B
1	FORMULA	RESULT
2	=TODAY()	7/13/2015
3	=NOW()	7/13/2015 10:28 AM

NetWorkDays

Syntax:

`NETWORKDAYS(start_date, end_date, [holidays])`

start_date and **end_date** are required, **holidays is optional**

C2			X	✓	f_x	=NETWORKDAYS(A2,B2)	

	A	B	C	D	E
1	START DATE	COMPLETION DATE	HOW MANY WORKDAYS?		
2	8/1/2015	10/31/2015	65		
3					

WEB ADDRESS & FILE NAME FOR EXERCISE:
http://bentonexcelbooks.my-free.website/excel-2016
NetWorkDays.xlsx

Scenario:

You've been asked to determine how many resources are needed to complete a project by specific date.

- The start of the project is 08/01/2015 and needs to be completed by 10/31/2015
- The project is estimated to take 1,040 hours
- Assume each resource would work one 8 hour shift per day, Monday – Friday

It would take 1 resource 130 days to complete the project including weekends:

$$(1040 \text{ hours} / 8 \text{ hour shift} = 130 \text{ days})$$

Therefore, we know we need more resources, but how many?

Step-By-Step Example:

First, we need to determine how many *workdays* there are between 08/01/2015 and 10/31/2015. Once we know this amount, we can then multiply this value with the number of hours per shift to determine the appropriate total of resources needed to complete the project by 10/31/2015.

1. Open the spreadsheet NetWorkDays.xlsx
2. Place your cursor in cell '**C2**'
3. From the Ribbon select the tab '**Formulas**'
4. In the '**Function Library**' section, click the drop-down box for '**Date & Time**'
5. Scroll-down and select '**NETWORKDAYS**'

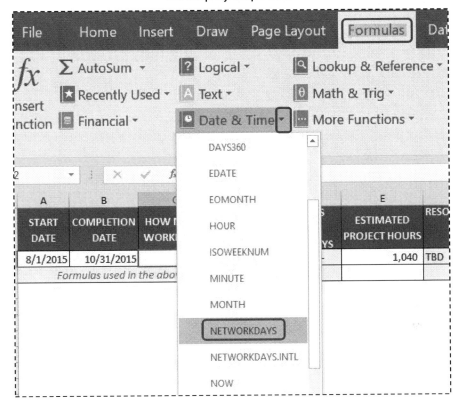

The following prompt will appear:

6. For the **Start_date** click cell '**A2**' or enter **A2**

7. For the **End_date** click cell '**B2**' or enter **B2**

8. Click the '**OK**' button

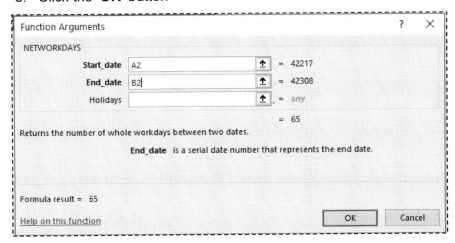

The result is **65 days:**

9. Apply the basic calculations to determine the appropriate amount of resources needed to complete the project (*please see screenshot below*)

(65 Days x 8 hours = 520 hours for 1 Resource)

(1040 hours/520 hours for 1 Resource = 2 Resources Needed)

	A	B	C	D	E	F
1	START DATE	COMPLETION DATE	HOW MANY WORKDAYS?	NUMBER OF HOURS WORKED FOR 1 RESOURCE FOR 65 DAYS	ESTIMATED PROJECT HOURS	RESOURCES NEEDED TO COMPLETE BY 10/31/2015
2	8/1/2015	10/31/2015	65	520	1,040	2
3	Formulas used in the above cells			C2*8 = 520		E2/D2 = 2

The result is **2 resources** are needed to complete a project by 10/31/2015.

CHAPTER 6

Conditional Functions

FUNCTION	DEFINITION
SumIF	Sums the values in a range based on the criteria you identify
AverageIF	Returns the average value (number) in a range of cells based on the criteria you identify
CountIF	Counts the number of times a value appears in a range of cells based on the criteria you identify
CountIFS	Counts the number of times a value appears in a range of cells based on the criteria you identify, *across multiple ranges*

Syntax:

SumIF:
SUMIF(range, criteria, [sum_range])

range and **criteria** are required, **sum_range** is optional

AverageIF:
AVERAGEIF(range, criteria, [average_range])

range and **criteria** are required, **average_range** is optional

CountIF:
COUNTIF(range, criteria)

range and **criteria** are required

CountIFS:
COUNTIFS(criteria_range1, criteria1, [criteria_range2, criteria2]…)

criteria_range1 and **criteria1** are required, additional **criteria ranges** and **criteria** are optional

Quick Examples:

	A	B	C	D	E	F	G	H	I
1	REGION	QTR	APPLES		QTR	SumIF	RESULT	AverageIF	RESULT
			SALES			FORMULA		FORMULA	
2	Central	1	235		Q1	=SUMIF(B:B,1,C:C)	884	=AVERAGEIF(B:B,1,C:C)	295
3	Central	2	285		Q2	=SUMIF(B:B,2,C:C)	1034	=AVERAGEIF(B:B,2,C:C)	344
4	Central	3	307		Q3	=SUMIF(B:B,3,C:C)	1166	=AVERAGEIF(B:B,3,C:C)	388
5	Central	4	367		Q4	=SUMIF(B:B,4,C:C)	1346	=AVERAGEIF(B:B,4,C:C)	449
6	East	1	272						
7	East	2	322						
8	East	3	410			*What are the total*		*What are the average*	
9	East	4	470			*sales by QTR?*		*sales by QTR?*	
10	West	1	377						
11	West	2	427						
12	West	3	449						
13	West	4	509						

	A	B	C	D	E	J	K	L	M
1	REGION	QTR	APPLES		QTR	CountIFS	RESULT	CountIF	RESULT
			SALES			FORMULA		FORMULA	
2	Central	1	235		Q1	=COUNTIFS(B:B,1,C:C,">400")	0	=COUNTIF(C:C,">400")	5
3	Central	2	285		Q2	=COUNTIFS(B:B,2,C:C,">400")	1		
4	Central	3	307		Q3	=COUNTIFS(B:B,3,C:C,">400")	2		
5	Central	4	367		Q4	=COUNTIFS(B:B,4,C:C,">400")	2	*How many times over all*	
6	East	1	272					*QTRs were sales greater*	
7	East	2	322					*than 400?*	
8	East	3	410			*How many times per QTR*			
9	East	4	470			*were sales greater than 400?*			
10	West	1	377						
11	West	2	427						
12	West	3	449						
13	West	4	509						

WEB ADDRESS & FILE NAME FOR EXERCISE:
http://bentonexcelbooks.my-free.website/excel-2016
SumIF_AverageIF_CountIF.xlsx

Scenario:
You've been given a spreadsheet that contains the Apple sales by quarter for three regions. You've been asked to summarize the data and provide the following information:

A. What are the **total** sales by quarter?

B. What are the **average** sales by quarter?

C. **How many times** per quarter were sales greater than $400?

D. **Total number of times** over *all* quarters, sales were greater than $400?

Step-By-Step Examples:

SumIF

A) What are the **total** sales by quarter?

1. Open the spreadsheet **SumIF_AverageIF_CountIF.xlsx**

2. Place your cursor in cell **'F2'**

3. From the Ribbon select the tab **'Formulas'**

4. Click fx **Insert Function**

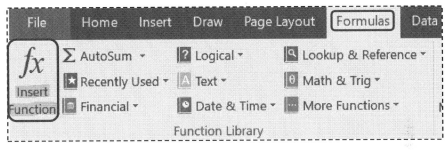

The following dialogue box will appear:

5. Type **'SumIF'** in the **'Search for a function:'** box

6. Click the **'Go'** button

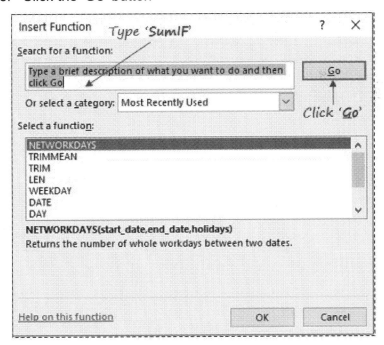

The following dialogue box should appear:
7. Click the '**OK**' button:

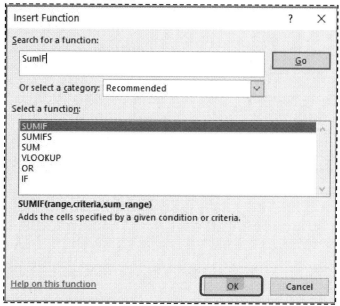

8. For the **Range** click the **column 'B'** *(this column lists the quarter)*

9. For the **Criteria** enter '**1**' for Quarter 1 *(note: if this were a text field, you would encapsulate the text with double quotes " ")*

10. For the **Sum_range** click the **column 'C'** *(this column list the Apple sales)*

11. Click the '**OK**' button

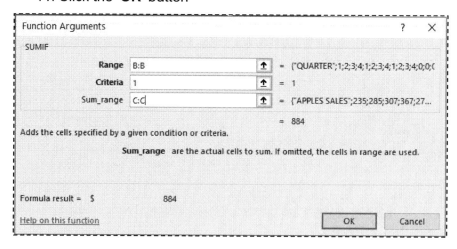

The result for **Q1** is **$884** sales:

12. Copy the formula down through cells **'F3' – 'F5'** and change the **'Criteria'** value for the appropriate quarter *(i.e. **2,3, & 4 for quarters 2-4**)*

E	F		E	F
QUARTER	**SumIF** Sales By QTR		QUARTER	**SumIF** Sales By QTR
Q1	=SUMIF(B:B,1,C:C)		Q1	$ 884
Q2	=SUMIF(B:B,2,C:C)		Q2	$ 1,034
Q3	=SUMIF(B:B,3,C:C)		Q3	$ 1,166
Q4	=SUMIF(B:B,4,C:C)		Q4	$ 1,346

Change the quarter number (Criteria)

AverageIF

B) What are the **average** sales by quarter?

1. Open the spreadsheet SumIF_AverageIF_CountIF.xlsx
2. Place your cursor in cell **'G2'**
3. From the Ribbon select the tab **'Formulas'**
4. Click *fx* **Insert Function**
5. When **'Insert Function'** prompt appears, type **'AverageIF'** in the **'Search for a function:'** box
6. Click the **'Go'** button

The following dialogue box should appear:
7. Click the '**OK**' button:

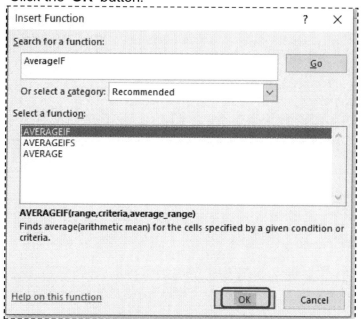

8. For the **Range** click the **column 'B'** *(this column lists the quarter)*

9. For the **Criteria** enter **'1'** for Quarter 1 *(note: if this were a text field, you would encapsulate the text with double quotes " ")*

10. For the **Sum_range** click the **column 'C'** *(this column list the Apple sales)*

11. Click the '**OK**' button

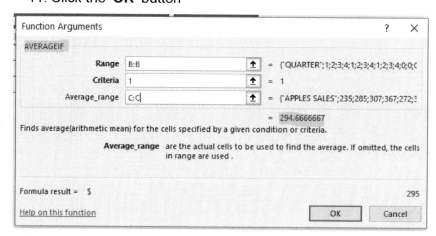

The result for **Q1** are average sales of **$295**:

12. Copy the formula down through cells '**G3**' – '**G5**' and change the '**Criteria**' value for the appropriate quarter (*i.e.* **2,3, & 4 for quarters 2-4**)

E	G		E	G
QUARTER	AverageIF Avg. Sales By QTR		QUARTER	AverageIF Avg. Sales By QTR
Q1	=AVERAGEIF(B:B,1,C:C)		Q1	$ 295
Q2	=AVERAGEIF(B:B,2,C:C)		Q2	$ 345
Q3	=AVERAGEIF(B:B,3,C:C)		Q3	$ 389
Q4	=AVERAGEIF(B:B,4,C:C)		Q4	$ 449

Change the quarter number (Criteria)

CountIFS

C) **How many times** per quarter were sales greater than $400?

*In this example, we need to determine two items 1) the quarter **AND** 2) the number of times sales were greater than $400*

1. Open the spreadsheet SumIF_AverageIF_CountIF.xlsx
2. Place your cursor in cell '**H2**'
3. From the Ribbon select the tab '**Formulas**'
4. Click *fx* **Insert Function**
5. When '**Insert Function**' prompt appears, type '**CountIFS**' in the '**Search for a function:**' box
6. Click the '**Go**' button

The following dialogue box should appear:
7. Click the '**OK**' button:

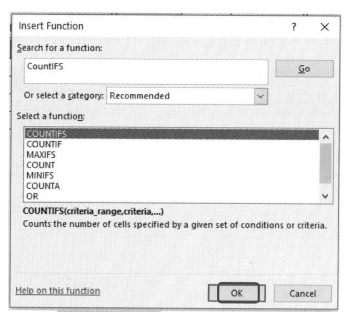

8. For the **Criteria_range1** click the **column 'B'** *(this column lists the quarter)*

9. For the **Criteria1** enter **'1'** for Quarter 1

10. For the **Criteria_range2** click the **column 'C'** *(this column list the Apple sales)*

11. For the **Criteria2** enter **">400"** for sales greater than $400, *(make sure $400 is in double quotes " ")*

12. Click the '**OK**' button

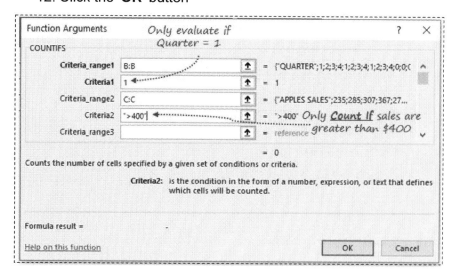

13. Copy the formula down through cells '**H3**' – '**H5**' and change the '**Criteria1**' value for the appropriate quarter *(i.e. **2,3, & 4 for quarters 2-4)***

	A	B	C	D	E	F	G
1	REGION	QTR	APPLES SALES		QTR	CountIFS Sales By QTR >$400	CountIFS Sales By QTR >$400
2	Central	1	235		Q1	=COUNTIFS(B:B,1,C:C,">400")	-
3	Central	2	285		Q2	=COUNTIFS(B:B,2,C:C,">400")	1
4	Central	3	307		Q3	=COUNTIFS(B:B,3,C:C,">400")	2
5	Central	4	367		Q4	=COUNTIFS(B:B,4,C:C,">400")	2
6	East	1	272				
7	East	2	322				
8	East	3	410				
9	East	4	470				
10	West	1	377				
11	West	2	427				
12	West	3	449				
13	West	4	509				

*Change the quarter number (**Criteria1**)*

Results that are = to 0 (zero) are displayed as a – (dash)

CountIF

D) <u>**Total number of times**</u> over *all* quarters, sales were greater than $400?

1. Open the spreadsheet SumIF_AverageIF_CountIF.xlsx

2. Place your cursor in cell '**J2**'

3. From the Ribbon select the tab '**Formulas**'

4. Click *fx* **Insert Function**

5. When '**Insert Function**' prompt appears, type '**CountIF**' in the '**Search for a function:**' box

6. Click the 'Go' button

The following dialogue box should appear:
7. Click the '**OK**' button:

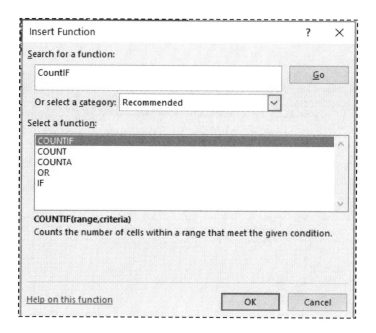

8. For the **Range** click the **column 'C'** *(this column lists the quarter)*

9. For the **Criteria** enter **">400"** for sales greater than $400, *(make sure $400 is in double quotes " ")*

10. Click the '**OK**' button

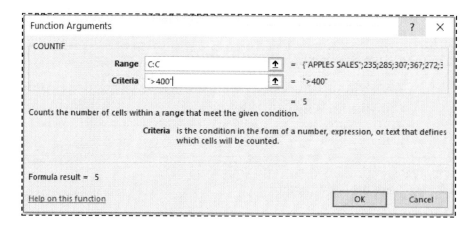

The result is **5**

| J2 | ▼ | : | × | ✓ | *fx* | =COUNTIF(C:C,">400") |

	A	B	C	E	F	G	H	J
1	REGION	QUARTER	APPLES SALES	QUARTER	SumIF Sales By	AverageIF Avg. Sales	CountIFS Sales By QTR	CountIF Sales >$400
2	Central	1	$ 235	Q1	$ 884	$ 295	-	5
3	Central	2	$ 285	Q2	$ 1,034	$ 345	1	
4	Central	3	$ 307	Q3	$ 1,166	$ 389	2	
5	Central	4	$ 367	Q4	$ 1,346	$ 449	2	

☑ Additional Information:

These functions may also be accomplished with Pivot Tables, which are introduced in the next chapter. However, sometimes it is quicker to use one of these formulas when your sample size is small or you're simply providing these results in an email, IM (instant message), or text.

CHAPTER 7

Pivot Tables & Pivot Charts an Introduction

What Are Pivot Tables?

Pivot Tables are a feature within Microsoft® Excel® that takes individual cells or pieces of data and lets you arrange them into numerous types of calculated views. These snapshots of summarized data require minimal effort to create and can be changed by simply clicking or dragging which fields are included in your report.

By using built-in functions and filters, Pivot Tables allow you to quickly organize and summarize large amounts of data. You can filter and drill-down for more detailed examination of your numbers and various types of analysis can be completed without the need to manually enter formulas into the spreadsheet you're analyzing.

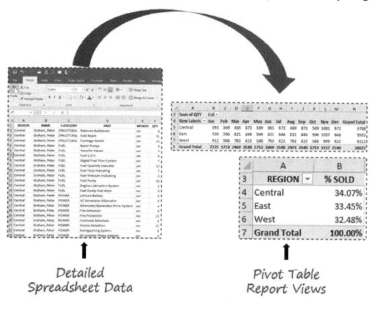

Detailed
Spreadsheet Data

Pivot Table
Report Views

For example, the below Pivot Table is based on a detailed spreadsheet of 3,888 individual records containing information about airplane parts. In less than 1 minute, I was able to produce the following report for the quantity of parts sold by region:

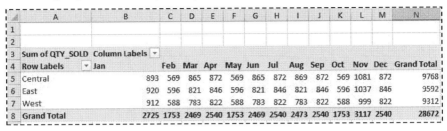

Sum of QTY_SOLD	Column Labels													
Row Labels	Jan	Feb	Mar	Apr	May	Jun	Jul	Aug	Sep	Oct	Nov	Dec	Grand Total
Central	893	569	865	872	569	865	872	869	872	569	1081	872	9768
East	920	596	821	846	596	821	846	821	846	596	1037	846	9592
West	912	588	783	822	588	783	822	783	822	588	999	822	9312
Grand Total	2725	1753	2469	2540	1753	2469	2540	2473	2540	1753	3117	2540	28672

In today's world where massive amounts of data is available, you may be tasked with analyzing significant portions of this information, perhaps consisting of several thousand or hundreds of thousands of records. You may have to reconcile numbers from many different sources and formats, such as assimilating material from:

- Reports generated by another application, such as a legacy system

- Data imported into Excel® via a query from a database or other application

- Data copied or cut and pasted into Excel® from the web or other types of screen scraping activities

- Analyzing test or research results from multiple subjects

One of the easiest ways to perform various levels of analysis on this type of information and more is to use Pivot Tables.

What Are The Main Parts Of A Pivot Table?

Before we begin our exercise, let's review the three main components of a Pivot Table:

1. **Rows:** The rows section typically represents how you would like to categorize or group your data. Some examples include: employee name, region, department, part Number etc.

2. **Columns:** The columns show the level or levels in which you're displaying your calculations. Often a *time period* such as month, quarter, or year, but can also be categories, product lines, etc.

3. **Values:** Values are the calculation portion of the report, these figures can be sums, percentages, counts, averages, rankings or custom computations.

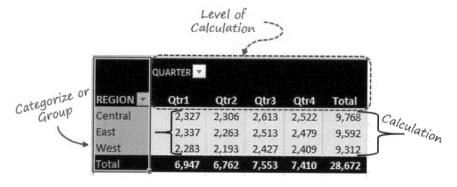

In this chapter we will review the fundamental steps of creating and modifying a Pivot Table. Here we will take a basic spreadsheet containing fruit sale information and:

A. Determine the total sales by region and quarter

B. Display the individual fruit sales by region and quarter

C. Create a chart that displays the sales by region and quarter

WEB ADDRESS & FILE NAME FOR EXERCISE:
http://bentonexcelbooks.my-free.website/excel-2016
FruitSales.xlsx

Step-By-Step Examples
How To Create a Pivot Table Report

Sample data, due to space limitations **the entire data set is not displayed**.

	A	B	C	D	E	F	G	H	I
1	REGION	SALES PERSON FIRST NAME	SALES PERSON LAST NAME	SALES PERSON ID	QUARTER	APPLES	ORANGES	MANGOS	TOTAL
2	Central	Bob	Taylor	1174	1	1,810	2,039	1,771	5,620
3	Central	Helen	Smith	833	1	102	354	59	516
4	Central	Jill	Johnson	200	1	93	322	54	469
5	Central	Sally	Morton	500	1	595	824	556	1,975
6	Central	Sam	Becker	800	1	863	1,092	824	2,779
7	East	Abbey	Williams	690	1	346	237	260	843
8	East	John	Dower	255	1	260	178	195	633
9	East	John	Wilson	300	1	286	196	215	696
10	East	Mary	Nelson	600	1	315	215	236	766
11	East	Sarah	Taylor	900	1	381	261	285	927
12	West	Alex	Steller	1000	1	163	212	127	502
13	West	Billy	Winchester	1156	1	179	234	140	552
14	West	Helen	Simpson	817	1	148	193	116	457
15	West	Jack	Smith	100	1	111	145	87	343
16	West	Joe	Tanner	400	1	122	160	96	377
17	West	Peter	Graham	700	1	134	175	105	415
18	Central	Bob	Taylor	1174	2	113	390	65	567
19	Central	Helen	Smith	833	2	1,006	1,393	940	3,338
64	West	Joe	Tanner	400	4	2,833	2,886	2,796	8,516
65	West	Peter	Graham	700	4	4,392	4,473	4,334	13,199

First, we will determine the 'total sales by region' and then we will build upon this by adding the 'quarterly sales by region':

1. Open the spreadsheet FruitSales.xlsx and highlight (select) cells A1:I65 *Please note: make sure to select cells 'A1:I65' and NOT the columns 'A:I'*

2. From the Ribbon select INSERT : PivotTable

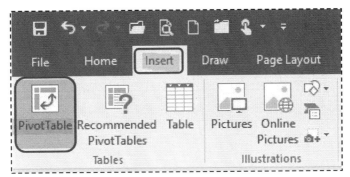

The following dialogue box should appear:

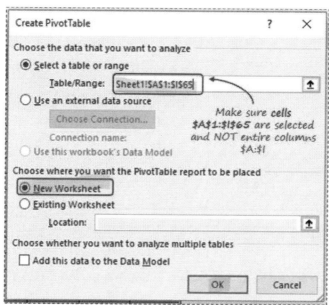

3. When prompted, verify the '**New Worksheet**' radio button is selected

4. Click the '**OK**' button

A new tab will be created and appear similar to the following. *Note: the 'PivotTable Fields' pane on the left side of the new worksheet.*

Next, we'll "categorize" our report and select a calculation value.

5. Inside the *PivotTable Fields pane* click the **'REGION'** box or drag this field to **'Rows'** section.

6. Inside the *PivotTable Fields pane* click the **'TOTAL'** box or drag this field to **'∑ Values'** section.

Please see image below, for an illustration of steps #5 & #6

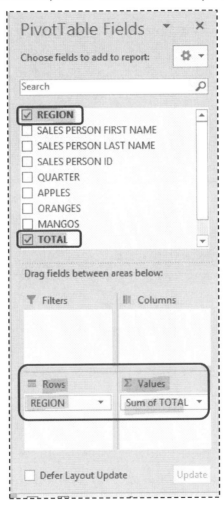

The following should be displayed on the right side of your screen
Note: the format is not very easy to read.

	A	B
1		
2		
3	Row Labels ▾	Sum of TOTAL
4	Central	138571.3795
5	East	145587.9689
6	West	196786.7115
7	Grand Total	480946.0598

7. We can change the column labels and format of the numbers. In the below example:

- Select cell **'A3'** and change the text from **'Row Labels'** to **'REGION'**

- Select cell **'B3'** and change the text from **'Sum of TOTAL'** to **'TOTAL SALES'**

- You may also change the currency format in cells **'B4:B7'**. In the below example, the format was changed to U.S. dollars with zero decimal places

Below is the formatted example:

	A	B
1		
2		
3	REGION ▾	TOTAL SALES
4	Central	$ 138,571
5	East	$ 145,588
6	West	$ 196,787
7	Grand Total	$ 480,946

To enhance the report, we're going to going add *Quarter columns*. This "level" dimension will provide greater detail of the total fruit sales.

8. Inside the *PivotTable Fields pane* drag the **'QUARTER'** field to the **'Columns'** section.

*Note: Excel® is reading the Quarter value as numeric, therefore if you **click, instead of drag this field** to the 'Columns' section, Excel® will apply a calculation.*

*If this happens click the drop down-box for **'Sum of QUARTER'** in the '∑ Values' section and select the option **'Move to Column Labels'***

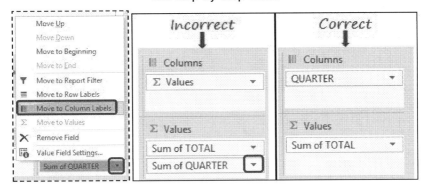

We now have **'QUARTER'** added to the summary

9. Select cell **'B3'** and change the text from **'Column Labels'** to **'BY QUARTER'**

10. The labels for cells **'B4'**, **'C4'**, **'D4'**, & **'E4'** were changed by adding the abbreviation text 'QTR' in front of each quarter number

Before *formatting:*

⊿	A	B	C	D	E	F
1						
2						
3	TOTAL SALES	Column Labels ▼				
4	REGION ▼	1	2	3	4	Grand Total
5	Central	$ 11,359	$ 19,352	$ 34,097	$ 73,763	$ 138,571
6	East	$ 3,865	$ 19,343	$ 38,811	$ 83,569	$ 145,588
7	West	$ 2,646	$ 23,586	$ 42,590	$ 127,964	$ 196,787
8	Grand Total	$ 17,870	$ 62,281	$ 115,499	$ 285,296	$ 480,946

After *formatting:*

TOTAL SALES	BY QUARTER ▼				
REGION ▼	QTR 1	QTR 2	QTR 3	QTR 4	Grand Total
Central	$ 11,359	$ 19,352	$ 34,097	$ 73,763	$ 138,571
East	$ 3,865	$ 19,343	$ 38,811	$ 83,569	$ 145,588
West	$ 2,646	$ 23,586	$ 42,590	$ 127,964	$ 196,787
Grand Total	$ 17,870	$ 62,281	$ 115,499	$ 285,296	$ 480,946

Adding Additional Rows (categories) To Your Pivot Table

From our original Pivot Table report, we'll extend our analysis by adding the individual fruit sales to our summary.

1. Drag the **'QUARTER'** field from the **'COLUMNS'** section to the **'ROWS'** section.

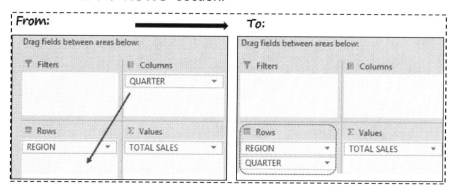

2. Drag the fields **'APPLES'**, **'ORANGES'**, & **'MANGOS'** to the **'VALUES'** section of the **PivotTable Fields** pane, place the fruit fields *before* the **'TOTAL SALES'** value

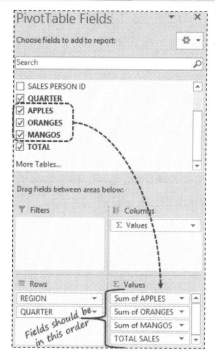

The results should look similar to the following:

REGION	Sum of APPLES	Sum of ORANGES	Sum of MANGOS	TOTAL SALES
⊟ Central	$ 43,481	$ 53,278	$ 41,812	$ 138,571
QTR 1	$ 3,463	$ 4,631	$ 3,264	$ 11,359
QTR 2	$ 5,992	$ 7,652	$ 5,709	$ 19,352
QTR 3	$ 10,634	$ 13,280	$ 10,183	$ 34,097
QTR 4	$ 23,392	$ 27,715	$ 22,656	$ 73,763
⊟ East	$ 50,626	$ 47,117	$ 47,845	$ 145,588
QTR 1	$ 1,587	$ 1,087	$ 1,190	$ 3,865
QTR 2	$ 6,891	$ 6,149	$ 6,303	$ 19,343
QTR 3	$ 13,583	$ 12,502	$ 12,726	$ 38,811
QTR 4	$ 28,564	$ 27,380	$ 27,625	$ 83,569
⊟ West	$ 69,750	$ 65,259	$ 61,778	$ 196,787
QTR 1	$ 856	$ 1,119	$ 671	$ 2,646
QTR 2	$ 7,819	$ 8,253	$ 7,513	$ 23,586
QTR 3	$ 15,335	$ 14,074	$ 13,182	$ 42,590
QTR 4	$ 45,739	$ 41,813	$ 40,411	$ 127,964
Grand Total	$ 163,857	$ 165,655	$ 151,435	$ 480,946

Charts - How To Create A Basic Pivot Table Chart

In our last example of this chapter, we'll review how to create and format a basic Pivot Table chart:

1. From the **PivotTable Fields** pane *uncheck* the '**TOTAL**' field

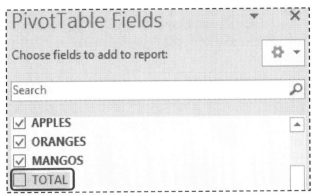

2. From the **PivotTable Tools** Ribbon select the tab **Analyze :
PivotChart**

Note: *If you do not see the **PivotTable Tools** option on
your Ribbon, click any PivotTable cell. This toolbar option
only appears when a PivotTable field is active.*

The following dialogue box should appear:

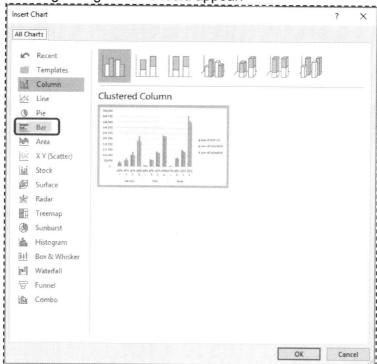

3. Select the **'Bar'** option
4. Click the **'OK'** button

A chart similar to the below should now be displayed:

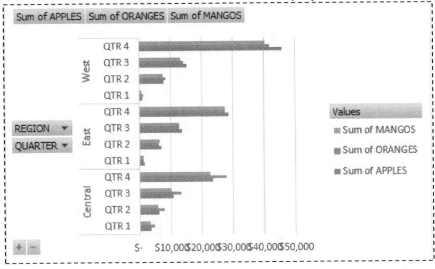

5. Drag the chart below the Pivot Table report summary and expand the width to allow for easier viewing

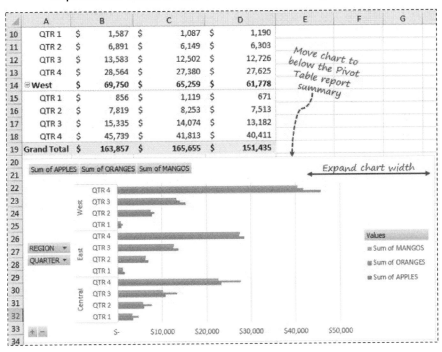

CHAPTER 8

How to Sort and Filter records

FEATURE	DEFINITION
Data Sorting	Allows you to change the order of rows in a spreadsheet to either *ascending (A – Z alphabetical)* or *descending (Z-A reverse alphabetical)*
AutoFilter	Allows you to easily navigate to specific records in a list. You may also use filtering to display or hide values on a report

WEB ADDRESS & FILE NAME FOR EXERCISE:
http://bentonexcelbooks.my-free.website/excel-2016
SortingAndFiltering.xlsx

Step-By-Step Example:
Data Sorting

Sample data, due to space limitations **the entire data set is not displayed**.

	A	B	C	D
1	FIRST NAME	LAST NAME	QUARTER	TOTAL
2	Helen	Simpson	1	$ 457
3	Helen	Simpson	2	$ 4,062
4	Helen	Simpson	3	$ 6,785
5	Helen	Simpson	4	$ 8,954
6	Billy	Winchester	1	$ 552
7	Billy	Winchester	2	$ 6,865
8	Billy	Winchester	3	$ 16,558
9	Billy	Winchester	4	$ 39,631
10	Peter	Graham	1	$ 415
11	Peter	Graham	2	$ 3,125
12	Peter	Graham	3	$ 5,969
25	Joe	Tanner	4	$ 8,516

1. Open the spreadsheet SortingAndFiltering.xlsx

2. Select cells 'A1:D25'

3. From the Ribbon select **Data : Sort**

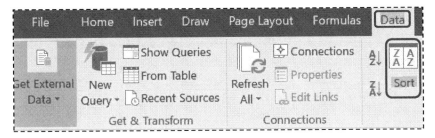

The following dialogue box should appear:

4. In the **'Sort by'** drop-down box select **'LAST NAME'** *(this is the primary sort)*. For the **'Order'** drop-down box select **'A to Z'**

5. Click the **'Add Level'** button, a new option called **'Then by'** will appear

6. In the **'Then by'** drop-down box select **'FIRST NAME'** *(this is the secondary sort)*. For the **'Order'** drop-down box select **'A to Z'**

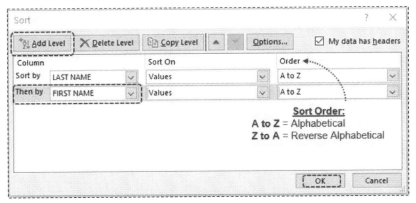

7. Click the **'OK'** button

You now have a list in alphabetical order by last name. Due to space limitations **the entire data set is not displayed**.

	A	B	C	D
1	FIRST NAME	LAST NAME	QUARTER	TOTAL
2	Peter	Graham	1	$ 415
3	Peter	Graham	2	$ 3,125
4	Peter	Graham	3	$ 5,969
5	Peter	Graham	4	$ 13,199
6	Helen	Simpson	1	$ 457
7	Helen	Simpson	2	$ 4,062
8	Helen	Simpson	3	$ 6,785
9	Helen	Simpson	4	$ 8,954
22	Billy	Winchester	1	$ 552
23	Billy	Winchester	2	$ 6,865
24	Billy	Winchester	3	$ 16,558
25	Billy	Winchester	4	$ 39,631

Additional Information:

NOTE: the check box **'My data has headers.'** Excel allows you to sort any range of cells. If this check box is *unselected* the **'Sort by'** drop-down options will appear as:

- Column A
- Column B
- Etc.

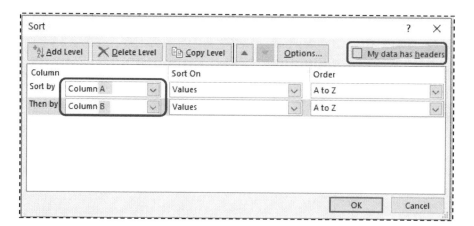

AutoFilter

1. Open the spreadsheet **SortingAndFiltering.xlsx**

2. Select (highlight) cells **'A1:D1'**

3. From the Ribbon select **Data : Filter**

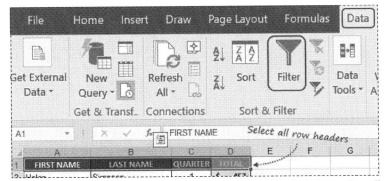

The following drop-down arrows should appear for each column heading:

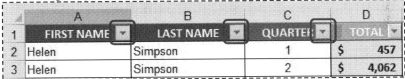

	A	B	C	D
1	FIRST NAME ▾	LAST NAME ▾	QUARTER ▾	TOTAL ▾
2	Helen	Simpson	1	$ 457
3	Helen	Simpson	2	$ 4,062

4. Click the down-arrow for **column 'C'** (QUARTER)

5. Uncheck the **(Select All)** box and click the box for Q1 **'1'**

6. Click the **'OK'** button

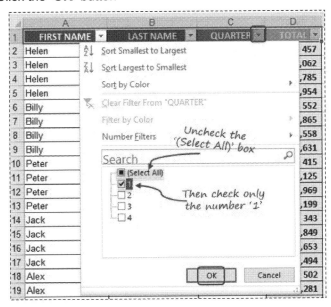

The following will be displayed, sales for 'Q1'

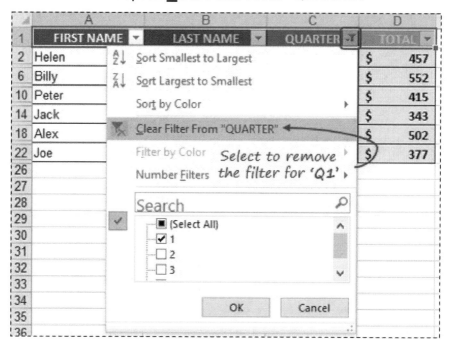

To **remove the filter**

7. Click the down-arrow for **column 'C'** (QUARTER)

8. Select the option **Clear Filter From "QUARTER"**

9. Click the down-arrow for **column 'D'** (TOTAL)

10. Click the option **'Number Filters'**

11. From the **'Number Filters'** menu, select the option **'Greater Than…'**

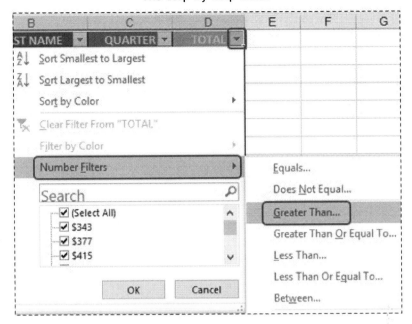

12. The following prompt will appear, enter **3000** in the box next to *'is greater than'*

13. Click the 'OK' button

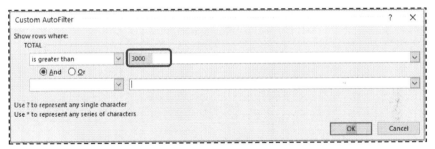

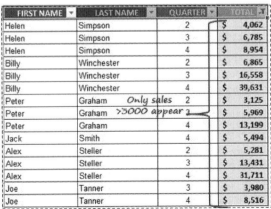

CHAPTER 9

Formula Display Utilities (troubleshooting tools)

Description:

- Formula trace is a graphical tool that can either identify all the cells a formula is referencing *or* all of the formulas (cells) the selected function is dependent on.

FEATURE	DEFINITION
Trace **Precedents**	Traces and displays graphically, with blue arrows, all of the cells a formula *is referencing (including)*
Trace **Dependents**	Displays graphically, with blue arrows, all of the formulas (cells) the selected function is **dependent on**

Quick Examples:

Trace **Precedents**

The formula in cell **'B3'** is *including values* in **cells 'A2', 'A4', & 'A5'**:

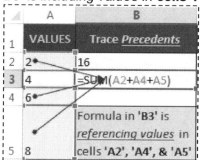

Trace **Dependents**

The formula in cell **'C3'** is *dependent* on the formula in **'B3'**:

	A	B	C
1	VALUES	Trace *Precedents*	Trace *Dependents*
2	2	16	20
3	4	=SUM(A2+A4+A5)	=B3*A3
4	6		
5	8		Formula in **'C3'** is *dependent on* the formula in **'B3'**

WEB ADDRESS & FILE NAME FOR EXERCISE:
http://bentonexcelbooks.my-free.website/excel-2016
FormulaAuditing.xlsx

Scenario:

The formula trace features within Excel® are an extremely helpful tool when you need to troubleshoot or validate a formula is calculating correctly, especially when troubleshooting complex formulas referencing many cells. Let's walk through a couple of examples:

- You've been contacted by a sales person who believes his sales are understated. He has asked you to verify his numbers are correct.

- A report used by sales managers has become increasingly difficult to read. You've been asked if there are some sections that can be deleted. To accomplish this without breaking *(effecting)* other formulas, you decide to use the Trace Dependents feature to ensure removing a particular section does not inadvertently effect other formulas.

Step-By-Step Examples:

Trace Precedents

Sample data, due to space limitations **the entire data set is not displayed**.

	A	B	C	D	E	F
1	FIRST NAME	LAST NAME	QUARTER	TOTAL		B. Winchester
2	Peter	Graham	1	$ 415		$ 63,606
3	Helen	Simpson	1	$ 457		
4	Jack	Smith	1	$ 343		
5	Alex	Steller	1	$ 502		
6	Joe	Tanner	1	$ 377		
7	Billy	Winchester	1	$ 552		
8	Peter	Graham	2	$ 3,125		
9	Helen	Simpson	2	$ 4,062		
10	Jack	Smith	2	$ 1,849		
25	Billy	Winchester	4	$ 39,631		
26						
27						

Precedents | Dependents | ⊕

The sales person Billy Winchester has asked you to verify his sales numbers of $63 606 are correct for the year.

1. Open the spreadsheet **FormulaAuditing.xlsx, select the tab 'Precedents'**

2. Place your cursor in cell **'F2'**

3. From the Ribbon select **Formulas : Trace Precedents**

A similar type of graphic should appear:

	A	B	C	D	E	F
1	FIRST NAME	LAST NAME	QUARTER	TOTAL		B. Winchester
2	Peter	Graham	1	$ 415		$ 63,606
3	Helen	Simpson	1	$ 457		
4	Jack	Smith	1	$ 343		
5	Alex	Steller	1	$ 502		
6	Joe	Tanner	1	$ 377		
7	Billy	Winchester	1	$ 552		
8	Peter	Graham	2	$ 3,125		
9	Helen	Simpson	2	$ 4,062		
10	Jack	Smith	2	$ 1,849		
11	Alex	Steller	2	$ 5,281		
12	Joe	Tanner	2	$ 2,404		
13	Billy	Winchester	2	$ 6,865		
14	Peter	Graham	3	$ 5,969		
15	Helen	Simpson	3	$ 6,785		
16	Jack	Smith	3	$ 2,653		
17	Alex	Steller	3	$ 13,431		
18	Joe	Tanner	3	$ 3,980		
19	Billy	Winchester	3	$ 16,558		
20	Peter	Graham	4	$ 13,199		
21	Helen	Simpson	4	$ 8,954		
22	Jack	Smith	4	$ 5,494		
23	Alex	Steller	4	$ 31,711		
24	Joe	Tanner	4	$ 8,516		
25	Billy	Winchester	4	$ 39,631		

F2 =D7+D13+D19+D25

We've now verified the sales for Billy Winchester are correct for the year.

Trace Dependents

Sample data, due to space limitations **the entire data set is not displayed**.

ANNUAL SALES								
CURRENT YR	Q1	Q2	Q3	Q4	ANNUAL	SALES PERSON	SALES	
Actual Sales	$ 2,646	$ 23,586	$ 49,375	$ 107,505	$183,113	Graham, Peter	$22,708	
Percent of Sales	1.4%	12.9%	27.0%	58.7%		Simpson, Helen	$20,258	
						Smith, Jack	$10,339	
	PROJECTED SALES					Steller, Alex	$50,925	
	Q1	Q2	Q3	Q4	ANNUAL	Tanner, Joe	$15,276	
1 YEAR	$ 2,779	$ 24,765	$ 51,844	$ 112,880	$192,268	Winchester, Billy	$63,607	
2 YEARS	$ 2,918	$ 26,003	$ 54,436	$ 118,524	$201,882			

A report used by sales managers has become increasingly difficult to read. They've asked you if the **'CURRENT YR Actual Sales'** *row* can be removed? You decide to use the **Trace Dependents** feature to ensure removing this particular section does not inadvertently effect other functions.

1. Open the spreadsheet FormulaAuditing.xlsx, select the tab 'Dependents'

2. Place your cursor in cell **'H3'**

3. From the Ribbon select **Formulas : Trace Dependents**

A graphic similar to the below will be displayed:

- We can see that cells **'H4'** & **'H8'** *(along with 'L4')* are *dependent* on cell **'H3'** which is part of the 'CURRENT YR Actual Sales' row.
- Therefore, if you were to remove this section it would adversely affect other formulas is this spreadsheet.

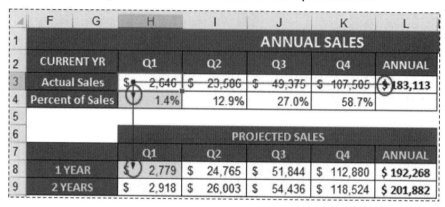

To **remove the arrows**, there are two options:

A. From the Ribbon select **Formulas : Remove Arrows** *or*

B. **Save** the spreadsheet

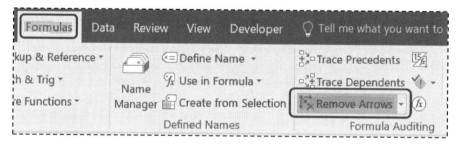

CHAPTER 10

How to unmerge records (Text-To-Columns)

FEATURE	DEFINITION
Text-To-Columns	Allows you to parse merged data from a single cell, fixed width, delimited, or structured file into separate Excel® columns

Scenario:

Often in my career I've had to parse information given to me from a source that has merged data elements together into a *single column*. Some of the most common examples are:

- Reports generated by another application *(often legacy systems)*. These reports are typically created in a **text (.txt)** or **comma separated file (.CSV)**.

- Data exported by a query from a database or other applications and pasted into Excel®.

- Data copied or cut and pasted into Excel® from the web or other types of screen scraping activities.

WEB ADDRESS & FILE NAME FOR EXERCISE:
http://bentonexcelbooks.my-free.website/excel-2016
EmployeeSales.xlsx

Step-By-Step Example:

Sample data:

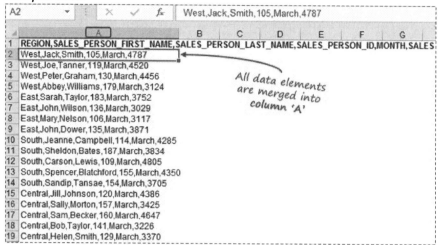

1. Open the spreadsheet EmployeeSales.xlsx

2. Click on **column 'A'**, *make sure the entire column is selected (highlighted)*

3. From the Ribbon select **DATA : Text to Columns**

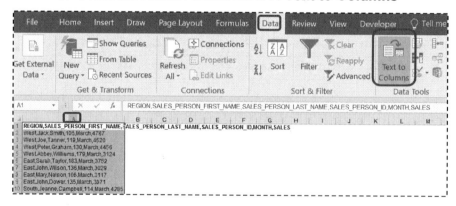

The following wizard will appear:

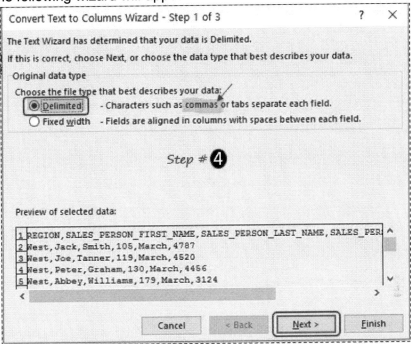

4. Select the '**Delimited**' radio button and click the '**Next>**' button

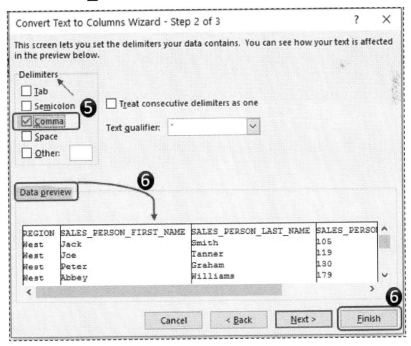

5. Select the '**Comma**' check box as your delimiter. ***Note** the 'Data preview' section. There are now separate columns of the what was the merged data in column 'A'*

6. If the data appears to be parsed correctly, click the '**Finish**' button

The merged data is now parsed into separate columns. Analysis or formatting may now be completed.

	A	B	C	D	E	F
1	REGION	SALES_Pl	SALES_Pl	SALES_Pl	MONTH	SALES
2	West	Jack	Smith	105	March	4787
3	West	Joe	Tanner	119	March	4520
4	West	Peter	Graham	130	March	4456
5	West	Abbey	Williams	179	March	3124
6	East	Sarah	Taylor	183	March	3752
7	East	John	Wilson	136	March	3029
8	East	Mary	Nelson	106	March	3117
9	East	John	Dower	135	March	3871
10	South	Jeanne	Campbell	114	March	4285
11	South	Sheldon	Bates	187	March	3834
12	South	Carson	Lewis	109	March	4805
13	South	Spencer	Blatchford	155	March	4350
14	South	Sandip	Tansae	154	March	3705
15	Central	Jill	Johnson	120	March	4386
16	Central	Sally	Morton	157	March	3425
17	Central	Sam	Becker	160	March	4647
18	Central	Bob	Taylor	141	March	3226
19	Central	Helen	Smith	129	March	3370

CHAPTER 11
Conditional Formatting

Feature:
- Conditional Formatting

Definition:
- Using different colors for cell shading and fonts, Conditional Formatting allows you to highlight cells based on specific criteria.

- Preset options include:
    - The Top & Bottom 10 *(the number 10 can be adjusted)*
    - The Top & Bottom 10% *(this percentage can also be adjusted)*
    - Above & Below the Average

- A very useful tool to quickly identify:
    - Duplicate values
    - A reoccurring date
    - Values greater or less than a specific number
    - Equal to a specific number
    - Cells that contain specific text

WEB ADDRESS & FILE NAME FOR EXERCISE:
http://bentonexcelbooks.my-free.website/excel-2016
MinAndMaxFormulas.xlsx

Scenario:
You've been given a spreadsheet that contains the total fruit sales by quarter and sales person. You've been asked to provide the *sales people* and *quarter* in which:

- Sales are greater than $10,000
- Sales are less than $1,000

Step-By-Step Example:
Sample data, due to space limitations **the entire data set is not displayed**.

	A	B	C	D	E	F	G
	SALES PERSON FIRST NAME	SALES PERSON LAST NAME	QUARTER	TOTAL		BEST SALES	WORST SALES
1							
2	Jack	Smith	1	$ 343			
3	Jack	Smith	2	$ 1,849			
4	Jack	Smith	3	$ 2,653			
5	Jack	Smith	4	$ 5,494			
6	Joe	Tanner	1	$ 377			
7	Joe	Tanner	2	$ 2,404			
8	Joe	Tanner	3	$ 3,980			
9	Joe	Tanner	4	$ 39,631			
25	Billy	Winchester	4	$ 8,516			

Conditional Formatting

1. Open the spreadsheet MinAndMaxFormulas.xlsx

2. Select cells in **column 'D' - 'D2 – D25'**

3. From the Ribbon select **HOME : Conditional Formatting**

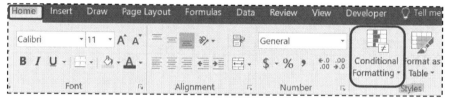

4. Select **Highlight Cells Rules > Greater Than...**

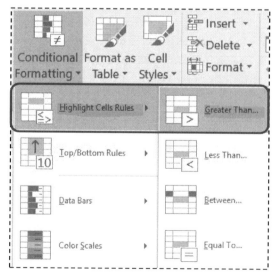

5. In the **'Format cells that are GREATER THAN':** box enter **10,000**

6. In the **'with'** box, click the drop-down box and select 'Green Fill with Dark Green Text'

7. Click the **'OK'** button

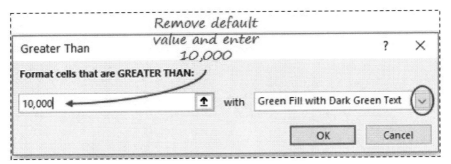

8. Repeat **steps 2 & 3** above

9. This time select **Highlight Cells Rules : Less Than...**

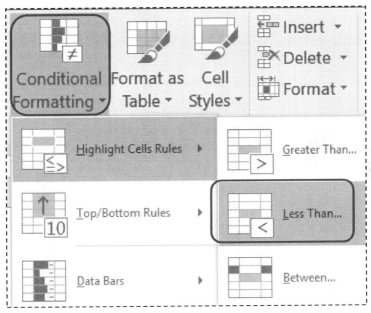

10. In the **'Format cells that are LESS THAN':** box enter **1,000**

11. In the **'with':** box click the drop-down box and select 'Light Red Fill with Dark Red Text'

12. Click the **'Ok'** button

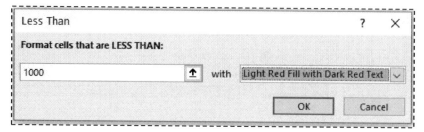

13. Highlight columns **'A' – 'D'**

14. From the toolbar select **DATA : Filter**

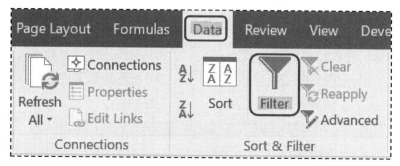

15. Click the filter drop-down arrow for **'TOTAL'** *(column 'D')*

16. Select **'Filter by Color':** **'Filter by Cell Color**

17. Select the green looking bar

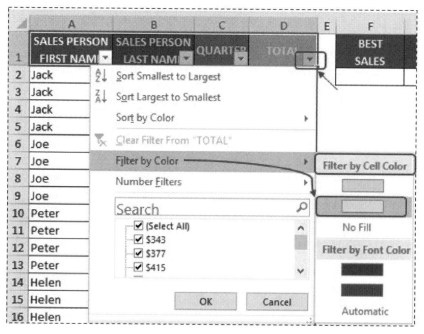

The following should now be displayed:

	A	B	C	D
1	SALES PERSON FIRST NAM ▼	SALES PERSON LAST NAM ▼	QUARTER ▼	TOTAL ⫫
9	Joe	Tanner	4	$ 39,631
13	Peter	Graham	4	$ 13,199
17	Helen	Simpson	4	$ 20,459
20	Alex	Steller	3	$ 13,431
21	Alex	Steller	4	$ 31,711
24	Billy	Winchester	3	$ 16,558

You've identified the quarter and sales people with sales greater than 10,000.

18. Click the filter drop-down arrow for '**TOTAL**' (column 'D')

19. Select '**Filter by Color**'

20. Select the red looking bar

The following should now be displayed:

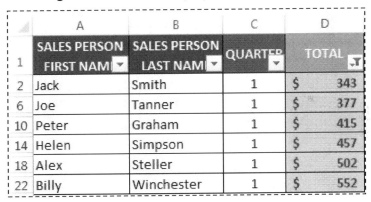

	A	B	C	D
1	SALES PERSON FIRST NAM ▼	SALES PERSON LAST NAM ▼	QUARTER ▼	TOTAL ⫫
2	Jack	Smith	1	$ 343
6	Joe	Tanner	1	$ 377
10	Peter	Graham	1	$ 415
14	Helen	Simpson	1	$ 457
18	Alex	Steller	1	$ 502
22	Billy	Winchester	1	$ 552

You've identified the quarter and sales people with sales less than 1,000.

Removing Conditional Formatting

To remove the Conditional Formatting:

1. From the Ribbon select **HOME : Conditional Formatting**:

2. Select '**Clear Rules**' and either option:
   a. Clear Rules from <u>S</u>elect Cells
   b. Clear Rules from <u>E</u>ntire Sheet

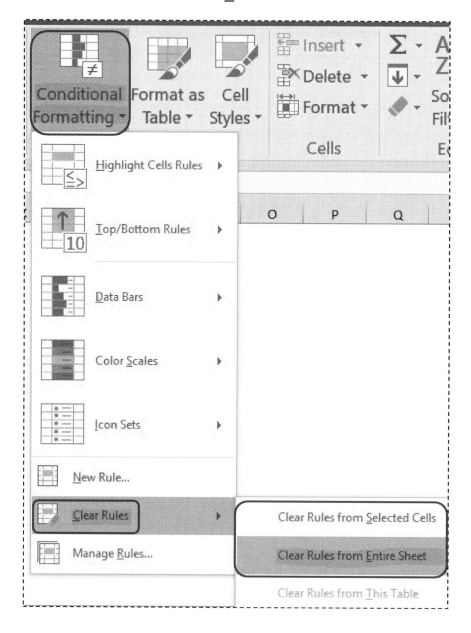

CHAPTER 12

Increase productivity with Data Validation

FEATURE	DEFINITION
Data Validation	Data validation allows you to create a drop-down list of values that can be entered into a cell. It effectively limits what is considered a *valid value* for a specific cell.

Data validation is an excellent tool to improve data quality, especially when multiple people access the same spreadsheet. **By using Data Validation you increase efficiency, consistency, and reduce typing errors**. For example, if you wanted to limit how a user entered a month value into a worksheet, you could use Data Validation to restrict the month entry to the three letter abbreviation *(please see the screenshot below)*:

A few more examples of how data validation may be used:

- **To limit numbers outside a specified range:** For example, you can specify a maximum bonus of 1% based on a sales number in a particular cell.

- **To limit dates outside a certain time frame:** For example, a date cannot be more than 365 days from today's date.

WEB ADDRESS & FILE NAME FOR EXERCISE:
http://bentonexcelbooks.my-free.website/excel-2016
DataValidation.xlsx

Scenario:

You're a Business Analysist in a Human Resources department and have been asked to provide a solution to a data entry problem with department managers accidentally *typing employee's names incorrectly and entering invalid values for total hours worked*. You decide to use Data Validation to resolve this problem.

Step-By-Step Example:

Data Validation

Sample data, due to space limitations **the entire data set is not displayed**.

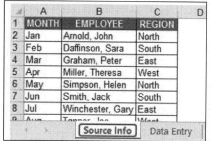 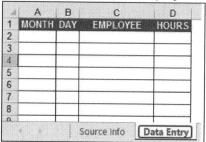

1. Open the DataValidation.xlsx spreadsheet
2. Select the tab named **'Data Entry'**

3. Click cell **'A2'**
4. From the Ribbon select **Data : Data Validation**

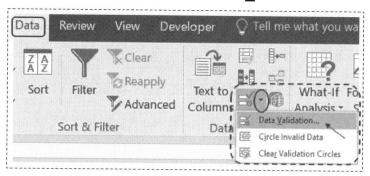

66

The following dialogue box should appear:

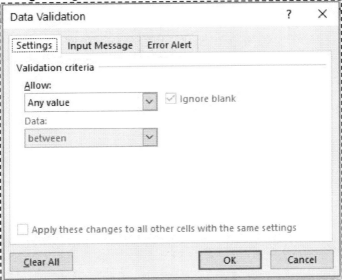

5. From the '**Allow:**' drop-down box select '**List**'

6. From the '**Source:**' box:
   - Click the '**Source Info**' tab
   - Select cells '**A2:A13**'

7. Click the '**OK**' button

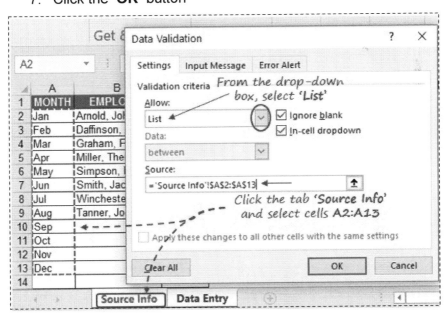

8. Return to the **'Data Entry'** tab, click on cell **'A2'**, note the drop-down box for month:

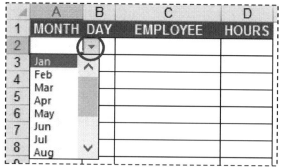

9. Click cell **'B2'** *(on the 'Data Entry tab)*

10. From the Ribbon select **Data : Data Validation**

11. From the **'Allow:'** drop-down box select **'Whole number'**

12. From the **'Data:'** drop-down box select **'between'**

13. Enter **1** in the **'Minimum:'** box

14. Enter **31** in the **'Maximum:'** box

15. Click the **'Input'** tab

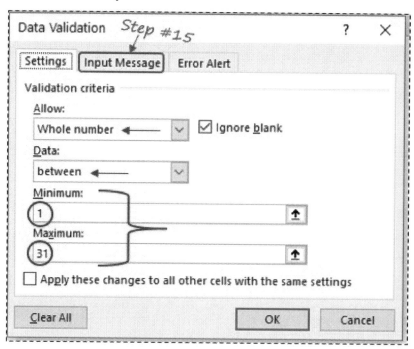

16. In the '**Title:**' box enter '**Day**'

17. In the '**Input message:**' box add the text '**Enter a number between 1 - 31**'

18. Click the '**OK**' button

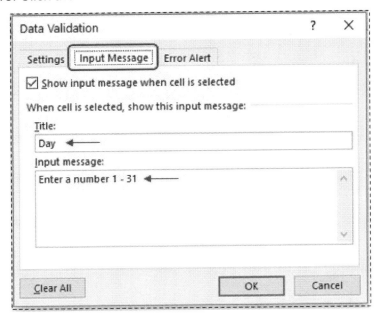

Note: when you click cell '**B2**' the following prompt appears:

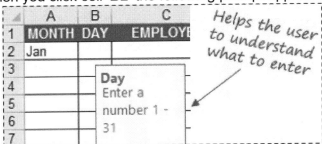

19. Click cell '**C2**' *(on the 'Data Entry tab)*

20. From the Ribbon select **Data : Data Validation**

21. Make sure the '**Settings**' *tab* is selected

22. From the '**Allow:**' drop-down box select '**List**'

23. From the '**Source:**' box:
    - Click the '**Source Info**' tab
    - Select cells '**B2:B9**'

24. Click the **'Error Alert'** tab

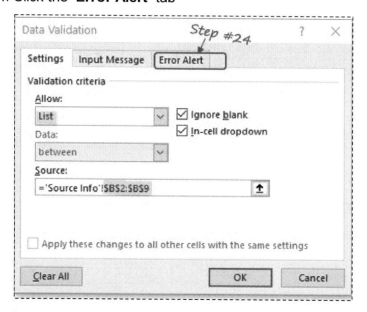

25. In the **'Title:'** box enter **'Employee'**

26. In the **'Error message:'** box add the text **'Employee Name Not Valid**

27. Click the **'OK'** button

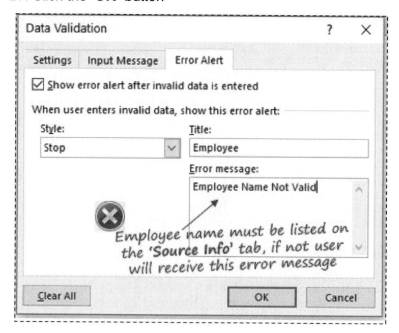

If the user enters a Employee name that is **not listed** on the 'Source Info' tab, they'll receive this error message:

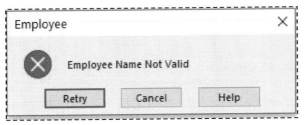

You may repeat steps #10 – 14 above for cell 'D2', to limit the valid hour entry to be between 1 – 8 hours:

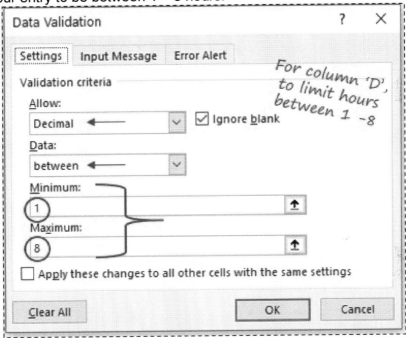

28. Select and **copy** cells **'A2:D2'** by pressing **(CTRL+C)** on your keyboard or:
    - From the Ribbon select the **'HOME'** tab
    - Click the **'Copy'** icon

29. Paste copied cells to **'A3:D15'**
    - Press **(CTRL+V)** on your keyboard _or_:
    - From the Ribbon select the **'HOME'** tab
    - Click the **'Paste'** button

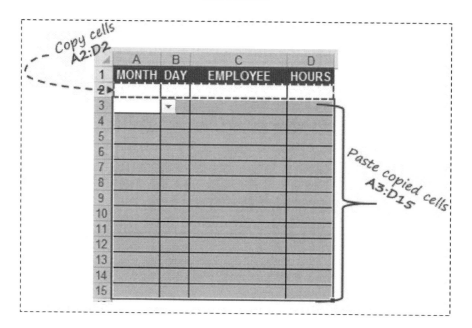

The completed form should appear similar to the following:

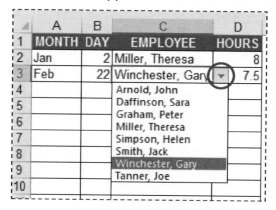

CHAPTER 13

Text Functions Part 1 - LEN & TRIM

FUNCTION	DEFINITION
LEN	The LEN function counts the number characters in a cell
TRIM	The TRIM function removes all extraneous spaces from a cell, except for single spaces between words

Quick Examples:

Syntax:
LEN(text)
text is required

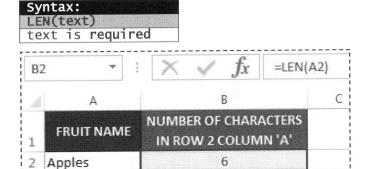

Syntax:
TRIM(text)
text is required

	A	B	C	D
1	FRUIT NAME	LEN COUNT OF CHARACTERS	TRIM FUNCTION	LEN COUNT OF CHARACTERS
2	Apples, Bananas, Mangos	27	Apples, Bananas, Mangos	23
3	Apples, Bananas, Mangos	23	Apples, Bananas, Mangos	23
4				

WEB ADDRESS & FILE NAME FOR EXERCISE:
http://bentonexcelbooks.my-free.website/excel-2016
TextFunctions.xlsx

Scenario:

You've been given a report that was created by a Database Administrator (DBA). The DBA created the file by running a query in a database, exporting the results into a .CSV file, and then opened and re-saved the report as an Excel® file.

As the Business Analyst, you're attempting to reconcile the data using a Pivot Table. In your analysis, you've discovered cell values that *"appear"* to be the same, but are being returned as two separate records in your results.

You use the LEN function to troubleshoot why you're getting two separate records in your results for what appear to be the same value.

Step-By-Step Examples:

LEN

Sample data:

	A	B
1	FRUIT NAME	FRUIT SALES
2	Apples	100
3	Kiwi	100
4	Oranges	100
5	Apples	200
6	Kiwi	200
7	Oranges	200
8	Apples	300
9	Kiwi	300
10	Oranges	300

1. Open the TextFunctions.xlsx spreadsheet

2. Select the tab named **'Len'**

3. Sort the results by **'Fruit Name'** in __Ascending order__ *(please see chapter 8 for instructions on Data Sorting)*

Sort Column 'A' in Ascending order

	A	B
1	FRUIT NAME	FRUIT SALES
2	Apples	100
3	Kiwi	100
4	Oranges	100
5	Apples	200
6	Kiwi	200
7	Oranges	200
8	Apples	300
9	Kiwi	300
10	Oranges	300
11		

4. Click cell **'C2'**

	A	B	C
1	FRUIT NAME	FRUIT SALES	LEN FUNCTION
2	Apples	100	
3	Apples	200	
4	Apples	300	
5	Kiwi	100	
6	Kiwi	200	
7	Kiwi	300	
8	Oranges	100	
9	Oranges	200	
10	Oranges	300	
11			

5. From the Ribbon select **Formulas : Text : LEN**

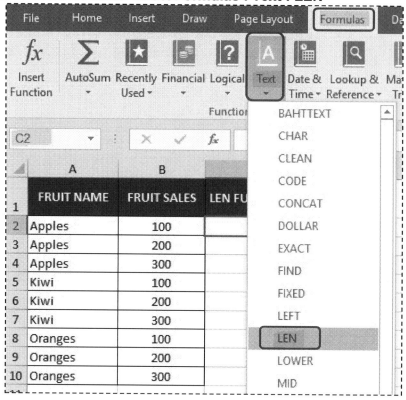

The following dialogue box will appear:

6. Click on cell '**A2**' or enter '**A2**' in the **Text** field
7. Click the '**OK**' button

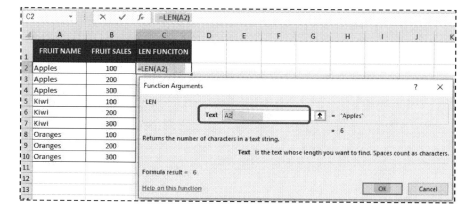

8. Copy the LEN formula down to cells '**C3:C10**'

There appears to be an extra space in cells '**A3**' & '**A4**' after the fruit name '*Apple*'

	A	B	C
1	FRUIT NAME	FRUIT SALES	LEN FUNCTION
2	Apples	100	6
3	Apples	200	7
4	Apples	300	7
5	Kiwi	100	4
6	Kiwi	200	4
7	Kiwi	300	4
8	Oranges	100	7
9	Oranges	200	7
10	Oranges	300	7

9. Remove the extra space in cells '**A3** & **A4**' at the end of the fruit name '**Apple**'

10. Save your changes

You would now be able to re-run your Pivot Table report and the results should appear correctly

3	Row Labels ▾	Sum of FRUIT SALES
4	Apples	600
5	Kiwi	600
6	Oranges	600
7	**Grand Total**	**1800**

TRIM

Scenario:

You've been given an Excel® report generated by another application. Upon review, you see the content in the cells contains extra spaces between and after the words. To make the report usable for analysis and presentation you need to remove the extraneous spaces. You decide to use the **TRIM function** to remove the spaces.

77

Below is an example of the report showing what must be corrected in order to create a Pivot Table report.

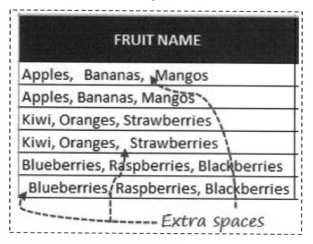

1.   Open the TextFunctions.xlsx spreadsheet

2.   Select the tab named **'Trim'**

3.   Click cell **'C2'**

	A	B	C
1	FRUIT NAME	LEN COUNT OF CHARACTERS	TRIM FUNCTION
2	Apples, Bananas, Mangos	27	
3	Apples, Bananas, Mangos	23	
4	Kiwi, Oranges, Strawberries	27	
5	Kiwi, Oranges, Strawberries	29	
6	Blueberries, Raspberries, Blackberries	38	
7	Blueberries, Raspberries, Blackberries	40	

4.   From the Ribbon select **Formulas : Text : TRIM**

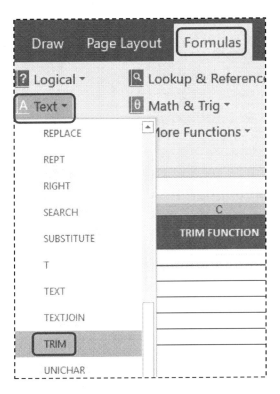

The following dialogue box will appear:

5. Click cell '**A2**' or enter **A2** in the **Text** field

6. Click the '**OK**' button

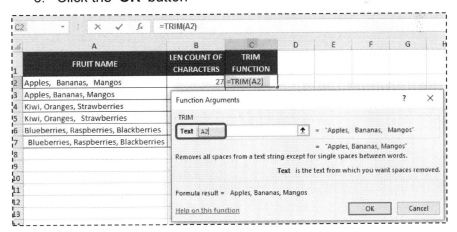

7. Copy the **TRIM** formula down cells '**C3:C7**'

8. The extra spaces have been removed

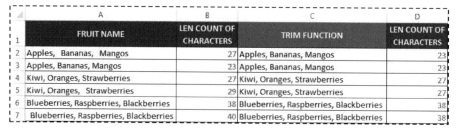

	A	B	C	D
1	FRUIT NAME	LEN COUNT OF CHARACTERS	TRIM FUNCTION	LEN COUNT OF CHARACTERS
2	Apples, Bananas, Mangos	27	Apples, Bananas, Mangos	23
3	Apples, Bananas, Mangos	23	Apples, Bananas, Mangos	23
4	Kiwi, Oranges, Strawberries	27	Kiwi, Oranges, Strawberries	27
5	Kiwi, Oranges, Strawberries	29	Kiwi, Oranges, Strawberries	27
6	Blueberries, Raspberries, Blackberries	38	Blueberries, Raspberries, Blackberries	38
7	Blueberries, Raspberries, Blackberries	40	Blueberries, Raspberries, Blackberries	38

Next we'll copy and **paste as values** *the contents of column C and remove the columns (B, C, D,& E) used for troubleshooting.*

9. Select cells '**C2:C7**'

10. Click the '**Copy**' button or press **CTRL+C** from your keyboard

11. Select cell '**A2**'

12. **Right-click** and select '**Paste Special...**'

13. Select the '**Values**' radio button

14. Click the '**OK**' button

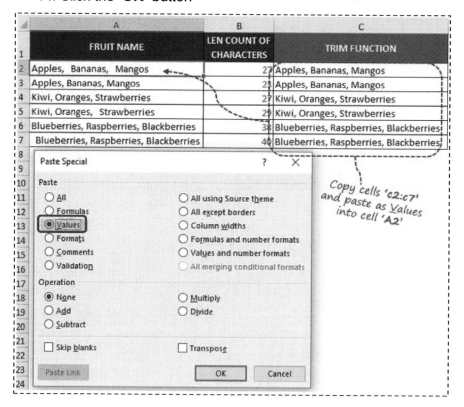

15. Select columns **'B', 'C', 'D', &'E'**

16. **Right-click** and select **'Delete'**, the troubleshooting columns B', 'C', 'D', &'E' should now be removed

We have successfully removed all extraneous spaces from the records contained in **column 'A'**. Further analysis and reporting can be completed without error.

	A	B
1	**FRUIT NAME**	
2	Apples, Bananas, Mangos	
3	Apples, Bananas, Mangos	
4	Kiwi, Oranges, Strawberries	
5	Kiwi, Oranges, Strawberries	
6	Blueberries, Raspberries, Blackberries	
7	Blueberries, Raspberries, Blackberries	

CHAPTER 14

Text Functions Part 2 - Proper, Upper, Lower, Concat, & Mid

FUNCTION	DEFINITION
PROPER	Converts the text of a cell to proper (normal case). The first letter of each word is uppercase (capitalized) and all other letters of the same word are lowercase
UPPER	Converts all text characters of a cell to **UPPERCASE** (capitalized)
LOWER	Converts all text characters of a cell to **lowercase**
CONCAT / CONCATENATE	Joins two or more cells together, also allows the option to insert additional text into the merged cell
MID	Returns a specific number of characters from a text string, starting at the position you specify, based on the number of characters you stipulate

Quick Examples:

Syntax:	Syntax:	Syntax:
PROPER(text)	UPPER(text)	LOWER(text)
text is required	text is required	text is required

⊿	A	B	C
1	FROM--->	FORMULA	TO
2	apples	=PROPER(A2)	Apples
3	Apples	=UPPER(A3)	APPLES
4	APPLES	=LOWER(A4)	apples

Function Syntax:	Function Syntax:	
CONCAT(text)	CONCATENATE(text)	*Excel version*
text is required	text is required	*2013 & earlier*

82

	A	B	C	D
	SALES PERSON FIRST NAME	SALES PERSON LAST NAME	FORMULA	Merged cells 'B2' & 'A2', Last Name, followed by a comma and space, then First Name
1				
2	Jack	Smith	=CONCATENATE(B2,", ",A2)	Smith, Jack

```
Syntax:
MID(text, start_num, num_chars)
All arguments are required
```

	A	B	C	D
	SALES PERSON FIRST NAME	SALES PERSON LAST NAME	FORMULA	Started in positon 1 of cell 'A2' and returned the 1st character
1				
2	Jack	Smith	=MID(A2,1,1)	J

WEB ADDRESS & FILE NAME FOR EXERCISE:
http://bentonexcelbooks.my-free.website/excel-2016
TextFunctions.xlsx

Step-By-Step Examples:
Proper

Sample data:

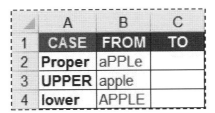

	A	B	C
1	CASE	FROM	TO
2	Proper	aPPLe	
3	UPPER	apple	
4	lower	APPLE	

1. Open the TextFunctions.xlsx spreadsheet

2. Select the tab named **'Case'**

3. Place your cursor in cell **'C2'**

4. From the Ribbon select **Formulas : Text**

5. From the drop-down list, select the option **'PROPER'**

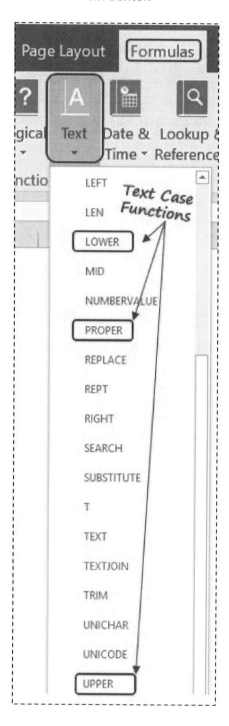

6. In the Function Arguments dialogue box, click cell **'B2'** or enter **B2** in the **'Text'** field

7. Click the **'OK'** button

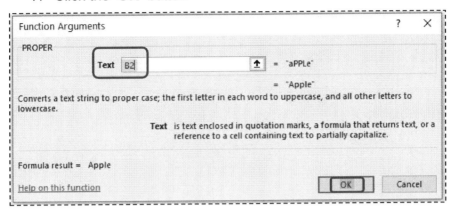

Upper

1. Place your cursor in cell **'C3'**

2. From the Ribbon select **Formulas : Text : Upper**

3. In the Function Arguments dialogue box, click cell **'B3'** or enter **B3** in the **'Text'** field

4. Click the **'OK'** button

Lower

1. Place your cursor in cell **'C4'**

2. From the Ribbon select **Formulas : Text : Lower**

3. In the Function Arguments dialogue box, click cell **'B4'** or enter **B4** in the **'Text'** field

4. Click the **'OK'** button

The result should be as follows:

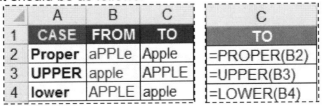

	A	B	C		C
1	CASE	FROM	TO		TO
2	Proper	aPPLe	Apple		=PROPER(B2)
3	UPPER	apple	APPLE		=UPPER(B3)
4	lower	APPLE	apple		=LOWER(B4)

Concat

<u>Scenario</u>:
You've been given a list of employees that need to be notified of a change in healthcare benefits. You've been asked to:

- Generate an email list based on these names

Sample data:

	A	B	C
1	FIRST NAME	LAST NAME	EMAIL ADDRESS
2	Billy	Winchester	
3	Helen	Smith	
4	Sally	Morton	
5	Jill	Johnson	
6	John	Dower	

1. Open the TextFunctions.xlsx spreadsheet

2. Select the tab named **'Concat'**

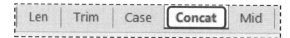

3. Place your cursor in cell **'C2'**

4. From the Ribbon select **Formulas : Text**

5. From the drop-down list, select the option **'CONCAT'**

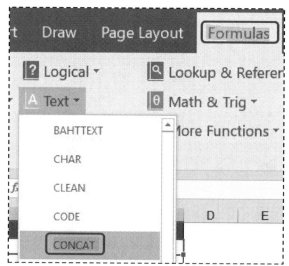

In the Function Arguments dialogue box enter the following:

6. **Text1** box click cell '**A2**' or enter **A2**

7. **Text2** box click cell '**B2**' or enter **B2**

8. **Text3** box enter the text **@fakecompany.com**

9. Click the '**OK**' button

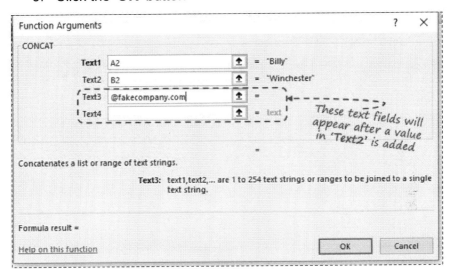

10. Copy the **CONCAT** formula down cells '**C3:C6**'

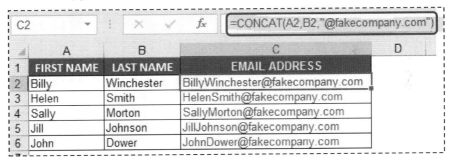

We now have an email list.

Concatenate (Excel® v2013 & earlier)

To use this functionality in Excel® v2013 & earlier:

1. From the Ribbon select **Formulas : Text**

2. From the drop-down list, select the option '**CONCATENATE**'

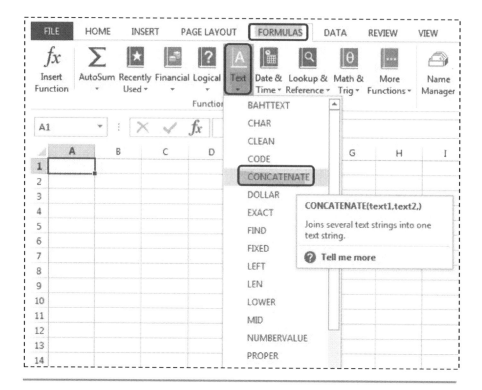

Alternatively, you may perform the same type of functionality WITHOUT using the formula wizard for CONCAT. Instead, by using the **ampersand (&) symbol**. This is how many intermediate and advanced Excel® users typically execute this command. Please see below for an example:

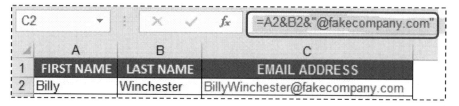

MID

Scenario

You've been given a list of stores from a database which prepends each location with three zeros. You need to add information from this list into an existing spreadsheet that _does not have_ the leading zeros for the stores. You plan on using the MID formula to:

- Return the store number *without* the three leading zeros

Sample data:

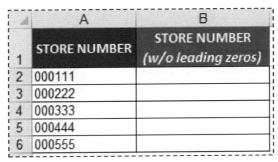

	A	B
1	STORE NUMBER	STORE NUMBER *(w/o leading zeros)*
2	000111	
3	000222	
4	000333	
5	000444	
6	000555	

1. Open the TextFunctions.xlsx spreadsheet

2. Select the tab named **'Mid'**

| Len | Trim | Case | Concat | **Mid** |

3. Place your cursor in cell **'B2'**

4. From the Ribbon select **Formulas : Text**

5. From the drop-down list, select the option **'MID'**

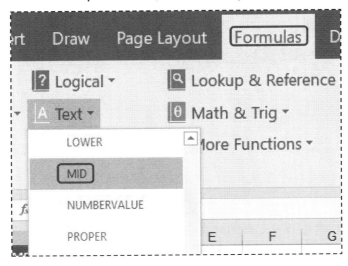

In the Function Arguments dialogue box enter the following:

6. **Text** box click cell '**A2**' or enter **A2**

7. **Start_num** enter the number **4**, *this is the position where the store number begins*

8. **Num_chars** enter the number **3**, *this is the number of characters to be returned*

9. Click the '**OK**' button

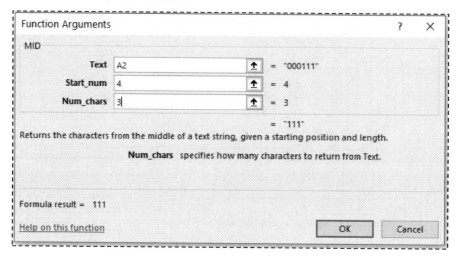

10. Copy the **MID** formula down to cells '**C3:C6**'

	A	B		B
1	STORE NUMBER	STORE NUMBER (w/o leading zeros)		STORE NUMBER (w/o leading zeros)
2	000111	111		=MID(A2,4,3)
3	000222	222		=MID(A3,4,3)
4	000333	333		=MID(A4,4,3)
5	000444	444		=MID(A5,4,3)
6	000555	555		=MID(A6,4,3)

We now have a list of store numbers without the three leading zeros.

CHAPTER 15

Logic tests – cell evaluation

FUNCTION	DEFINITION
IF	IF formulas allow you test conditions and return one value *if true* and another *if false*
AND	AND formulas allow you test multiple conditions and return a value of **'TRUE'** *if all* conditions are true otherwise the value **'FALSE'** is returned

Quick Examples:

IF - Syntax:

IF(logical_test, value_if_true, [value_if_false])

logic_test required, **value_if_true** required, **value_if_false** optional

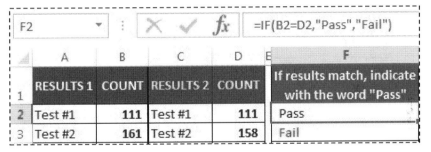

F2		✕ ✓ *fx*	=IF(B2=D2,"Pass","Fail")		
▲	A	B	C	D	E	F
1	RESULTS 1	COUNT	RESULTS 2	COUNT	If results match, indicate with the word "Pass"
2	Test #1	111	Test #1	111	Pass
3	Test #2	161	Test #2	158	Fail

AND - Syntax:

AND(logical_test1, logical_test2,…)

logic_test1 required, **logic_test2** required

D2		✕ ✓ *fx*	=AND(B2>=480,C2<=4)
▲	A	B	C	D	E
1	SALES PERSON	HOURS	ABSENCES	Bonus Eligible?
2	Graham, Peter	484	3	TRUE
3	Simpson, Helen	480	3	TRUE
4	Smith, Jack	482	7	FALSE

Associates must have worked a minimum of 480 hours AND had no more than 4 absences

91

Scenario:

You're a data analyst working on a project and need to compare test results:

a. If the results match between the two datasets, insert the text **'Pass'**

b. If the results DO NOT match, insert the text **'Fail'**

Step-By-Step Examples:

IF

Sample data:

⬜	A	B	C	D	E	F
1	RESULTS A	COUNT	RESULTS B	COUNT		IF the results match, indicate with the text "Pass", otherwise use the text "Fail"
2	Test #1	111	Test #1	111		
3	Test #2	161	Test #2	158		
4	Test #3	183	Test #3	175		
5	Test #4	243	Test #4	243		
6	Test #5	263	Test #5	260		

1. Open the LogicExamples.xlsx spreadsheet

2. Select the tab named **'IF'**

3. Place your cursor in cell **'F2'**

4. From the Ribbon select **Formulas : Logical**

5. From the drop-down list, select the option **'IF'**

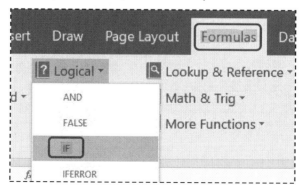

6. In the Function Arguments dialogue box enter the following:

   Logical_test   B2=D2
   Value_if_true   "Pass"
   Value_if_false "Fail"

7. Click the '**OK**' button

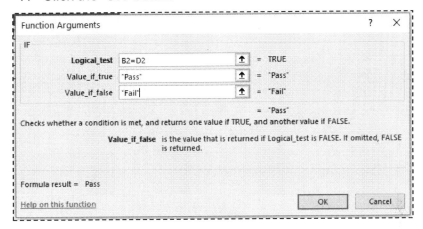

8. Copy the formula to cells '**F3:F6**'

The result should look similar to the following:

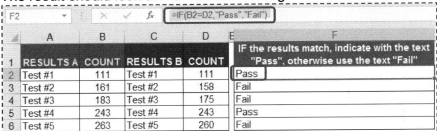

We've now compared two datasets and indicated if the results passed or failed.

AND

Scenario:

You're an accountant and need to determine if a Sales Associate is eligible for a bonus. Eligibility is based on the following criteria:

    a. The Sales Associate must have worked a minimum of 480 hours **_AND_**

    b. Had no more than 4 absences

Sample data:

	A	B	C	D
1	SALES PERSON	HOURS	ABSENCES	Bonus Eligible?
2	Graham, Peter	484	3	
3	Simpson, Helen	480	3	
4	Smith, Jack	482	7	
5	Steller, Alex	481	4	
6	Tanner, Joe	448	2	
7	Winchester, Billy	481	5	

1. Open the LogicExamples.xlsx spreadsheet
2. Select the tab named **'AND'**

3. Place your cursor in cell **'D2'**
4. From the Ribbon select **Formulas : Logical**
5. From the drop-down list, select the option **'AND'**

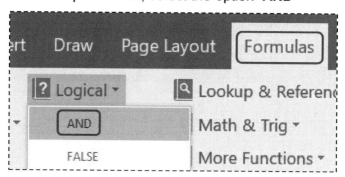

6. In the Function Arguments dialogue box enter the following:
   a. **Logical1** B2>=480
   b. **Logical2** C2<=4
7. Click the '**OK**' button

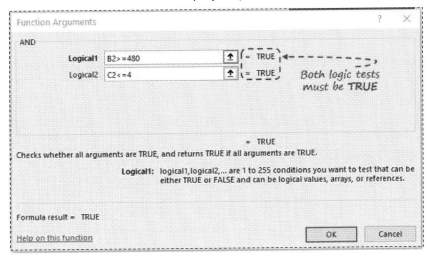

8. Copy the formula to cells '**D3:D7**'

The result should look similar to the following:

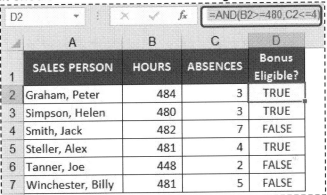

We've now determined the Sales Associates who are bonus eligible

Combining IF & AND Functions

Example of combining the **IF** & **AND** functions:

```
=IF(AND(B2>=480,C2<=4),"Yes","No")
```

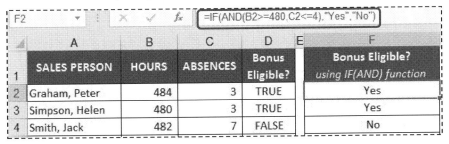

CHAPTER 16

VLOOKUP

FUNCTION	DEFINITION
VLOOKUP	The VLOOKUP formula allows you to vertically search for a value from one Excel® list and return that specific value to a new Excel® list, based on a matching lookup value

Quick Example:

```
Syntax:

VLOOKUP (lookup_value, table_array, col_index_num,
[range_lookup])

All parameters are required, except for
[range_lookup]
```

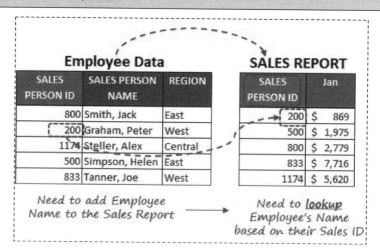

Employee Data

SALES PERSON ID	SALES PERSON NAME	REGION
800	Smith, Jack	East
200	Graham, Peter	West
1174	Steller, Alex	Central
500	Simpson, Helen	East
833	Tanner, Joe	West

SALES REPORT

SALES PERSON ID	Jan
200	$ 869
500	$ 1,975
800	$ 2,779
833	$ 7,716
1174	$ 5,620

Need to add Employee Name to the Sales Report

Need to lookup Employee's Name based on their Sales ID

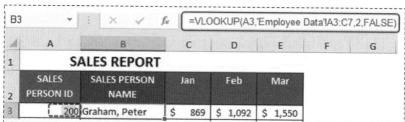

B3   fx   =VLOOKUP(A3,'Employee Data'!A3:C7,2,FALSE)

	A	B	C	D	E	F	G
1		**SALES REPORT**					
2	SALES PERSON ID	SALES PERSON NAME	Jan	Feb	Mar		
3	200	Graham, Peter	$ 869	$ 1,092	$ 1,550		

The 4 - parts of a VLOOKUP

❶ lookup value:

This is the field you want to find (match) typically located on another tab or spreadsheet.

In the example below, '**A2**' is selected, which has the Sales Person ID value of '**200**'. I will look to match this value on the tab labeled '**Sheet2**'. Sales Person Name is the value I want to look-up and be returned to the tab labeled '**Sheet1**'.

❷ table array:

This is the spreadsheet (tab) and range of cells searched for the ❶ lookup_value. The field you want to match must be in the first column of the range of cells you specify in the ❷ table_array.

In the example below, I'm searching the tab labeled '**Sheet2**' with the cell range of '**A2:B6**'.

❸ col index num:

Is the column containing the value you want returned.

In the example below, column '**2**' of the tab labeled '**Sheet2**' contains value of Sales Person Name which I want returned to the tab labeled '**Sheet1**'.

❹ range lookup:

Is the optional value of '**TRUE**' or '**FALSE**'. The value of '**FALSE**' would return an exact match, while '**TRUE**' would return an approximate match. Most users enter '**FALSE**' for this parameter.

Below, I have entered '**FALSE**' for an exact match.

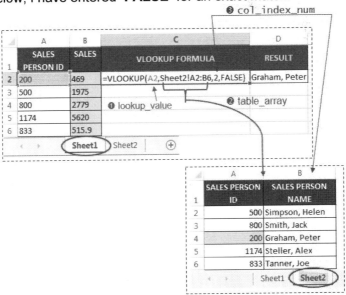

Scenario:

You've been asked to provide a list of the first quarter sales by month for each sales person. You run a query from the sales database and generate an Excel® report. Unfortunately, the database only contains the sales person's ID, *but not their name*. You use a VLOOKUP formula to pull the Sales Person's Name from an existing Excel® spreadsheet to the new sales report.

Step-By-Step Example:

VLOOKUP (how-to-use)
Sample data:

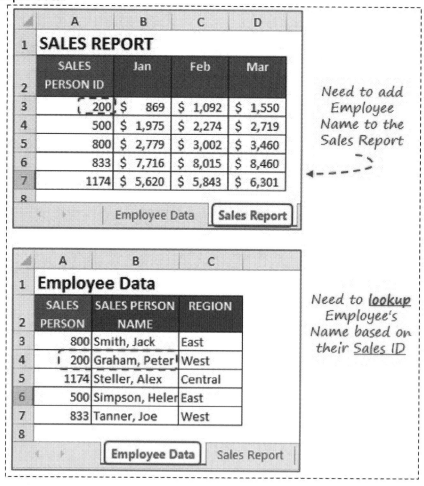

1. Open the Vlookup.xlsx spreadsheet

2. Select the tab named **'Sales Report'**

3. Place your cursor in cell **'B3'**

4. From the Ribbon select **Formulas : Lookup & Reference**

5. From the drop-down list, select the option **'VLOOKUP'**

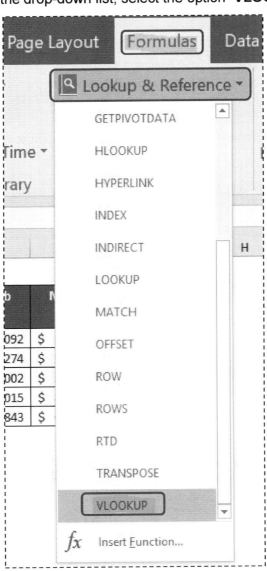

6. In the Function Arguments dialogue box enter the following:
   a. Click cell '**A3**' or enter **A3** in the dialogue box for the '**Lookup_value**' *(the sales person ID is the field we'll lookup on 'Employee Data')*

   b. For '**Table_array**', click on the tab '**Employee Data**' and select cells '**A3:C7**' *(this is the range of cells we're searching)*

   c. Enter the number **2** for '**Col_index_num**' *(this is the column containing the sales person's name)*

   d. For '**Range_lookup**' enter **FALSE**

7. Click the '**OK**' button

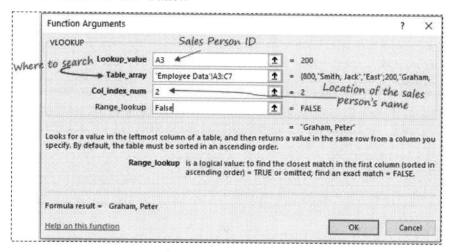

The following should be the result on the **Sales Report**:

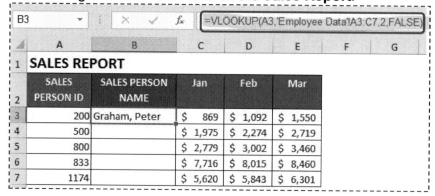

8. We need to do one additional step before we can copy this formula down to cells '**B4:B7**', we must add the U.S. dollar symbol **$** to the '**Table_array**'. This will prevent our cell range *(Table_array)* from changing:

```
=VLOOKUP(A3,'Employee Data'!$A$3:$C$7,2,FALSE)
```

If we attempted to copy the VLOOKUP formula to cells '**B4:B7**' without adding the **$**, the result would be as follows, **<u>NOTE:</u>** *how the* '*Table_array*' *cell range changes:*

	A	B
1	**SALES REPORT**	
2	SALES PERSO	SALES PERSON NAME
3	200	=VLOOKUP(A3,'Employee Data'!A3:C7,2,FALSE)
4	500	=VLOOKUP(A4,'Employee Data'!A4:C8,2,FALSE)
5	800	=VLOOKUP(A5,'Employee Data'!A5:C9,2,FALSE)
6	833	=VLOOKUP(A6,'Employee Data'!A6:C10,2,FALSE)
7	1174	=VLOOKUP(A7,'Employee Data'!A7:C11,2,FALSE)

Table_array changes

We would also receive a #N/A error in cells '**B5**' & '**B7**'

	A	B	C	D	E
1	**SALES REPORT**				
2	SALES PERSON ID	SALES PERSON NAME	Jan	Feb	Mar
3	200	Graham, Peter	$ 869	$ 1,092	$ 1,550
4	500	Simpson, Helen	$ 1,975	$ 2,274	$ 2,719
5	800	#N/A	$ 2,779	$ 3,002	$ 3,460
6	833	Tanner, Joe	$ 7,716	$ 8,015	$ 8,460
7	1174	#N/A	$ 5,620	$ 5,843	$ 6,301

9. After adding the **$** to the '**Table_array**', copy the VLOOKUP formula to cells '**B4:B7**'

```
=VLOOKUP(A3,'Employee Data'!$A$3:$C$7,2,FALSE)
```

We have successfully looked-up and added the Sales Person Name to the quarterly sales report. We can now provide a list of the first quarter sales by month for each sales person.

	A	B	C	D	E
1	SALES REPORT				
2	SALES PERSON ID	SALES PERSON NAME	Jan	Feb	Mar
3	200	Graham, Peter	$ 869	$ 1,092	$ 1,550
4	500	Simpson, Helen	$ 1,975	$ 2,274	$ 2,719
5	800	Smith, Jack	$ 2,779	$ 3,002	$ 3,460
6	833	Tanner, Joe	$ 7,716	$ 8,015	$ 8,460
7	1174	Steller, Alex	$ 5,620	$ 5,843	$ 6,301

	A	B	C	D	E
1	SALES REPORT				
2	SALES PERSON ID	SALES PERSON NAME	Jan	Feb	Mar
3	200	=VLOOKUP(A3,'Employee Data'!$A$3:$C$7,2,FALSE)	869	1092	1550
4	500	=VLOOKUP(A4,'Employee Data'!$A$3:$C$7,2,FALSE)	1975	2274	2719
5	800	=VLOOKUP(A5,'Employee Data'!$A$3:$C$7,2,FALSE)	2779	3002	3460
6	833	=VLOOKUP(A6,'Employee Data'!$A$3:$C$7,2,FALSE)	7715.9	8014.9	8459.9
7	1174	=VLOOKUP(A7,'Employee Data'!$A$3:$C$7,2,FALSE)	5620	5843	6301

Alternatively, for the **'Table_array'**, you may enter the columns **A:C** (Employee Data !A:C) instead of the range of cells (Employee Data!$A$3:$C$7), if the *entire column* contains the data you want returned, this would eliminate the need to complete **step 8**. However, depending on the number of records you're looking up *(the size of your data sample)*, there could be a reduction in performance speed when selecting the entire column. Especially, when using multiple functions together, for example combining a Nested IF and VLOOKUP.

Please see the below screenshots for a complete example using columns instead of cell ranges:

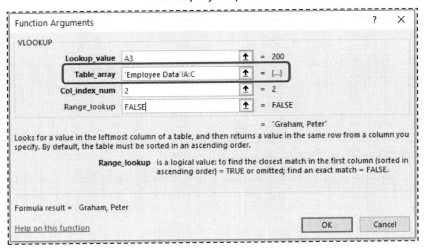

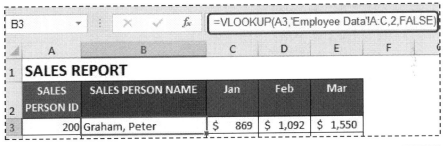

SALES PERSON ID	SALES PERSON NAME	Jan	Feb	Mar
	SALES REPORT			
200	=VLOOKUP(A3,'Employee Data'!A:C,2,FALSE)	869	1092	1550
500	=VLOOKUP(A4,'Employee Data'!A:C,2,FALSE)	1975	2274	2719
800	=VLOOKUP(A5,'Employee Data'!A:C,2,FALSE)	2779	3002	3460
833	=VLOOKUP(A6,'Employee Data'!A:C,2,FALSE)	7715.9	8014.9	8459.9
1174	=VLOOKUP(A7,'Employee Data'!A:C,2,FALSE)	5620	5843	6301

Excel Shortcuts &Tips

The following lists some of the most common Microsoft® Excel® shortcuts:

Shortcuts

DESCRIPTION	COMMANDS
FORMATTING	
CTRL+B	Applies or removes **bold** formatting
CTRL+I	Applies or removes *italic* formatting
CTRL+U	Applies or removes underlining formatting
FUNCTION	
CTRL+A	Selects (highlights) the entire worksheet
CTRL+C	Copies the contents of selected (highlighted) cells
CTRL+X	Cuts the selected cells
CTRL+V	Pastes the contents of selected (highlighted) cut or copied cells, including cell formatting
CTRL+F	Displays the Find and Replace dialog box, with the **Find** tab selected
CTRL+H	Displays the Find and Replace dialog box, with the **Replace** tab selected
CTRL+K	Displays the Insert Hyperlink dialog box for new hyperlinks or the Edit Hyperlink dialog box for selected existing hyperlinks
CTRL+N	Creates a new blank workbook
CTRL+O	Displays the dialog box to open a file
CTRL+S	Saves the active file with its current file name, location, and file format
CTRL+P	Displays the Print dialog box
CTRL+Z	The undo function will reverse the last command or to delete the last entry you typed
ESC	Cancels an entry in the active cell or 'Formula Bar'

NAVIGATION	
CTRL+PageUp	Switches between worksheet tabs, from **left-to-right**
CTRL+PageDown	Switches between worksheet tabs, from **right-to-left**
CTRL+↓	Goes to the last row with content for the active column
CTRL+↑	Goes to the first row with content for the active column
CTRL+→	Goes to the last column with content for the active row
CTRL+Home	Goes to cell A1 of the active worksheet
Shift + F3	Opens the Insert Function window
EDITING	
F7	Runs Spellcheck
Shift + F7	Opens the thesaurus dialogue box

Currency Formatting

Below are two ways to change a currency symbol. The following two examples demonstrate the **British Pound £** and **Euro €**:

1. Select the cells you would like to change the currency, in this example, cells '**B2**' – '**B6**' are highlighted:

	A	B	C
1	US	British Pound	Euro
2	$ 100	100	100
3	$ 200	200	200
4	$ 300	300	300
5	$ 400	400	400
6	$ 500	500	500

2. From the Ribbon select tab '**Home**' and click the drop-down box for **$**

3. Select one of the currency's listed, in this example, '**£ English (United Kingdom)**' was selected

Alternatively, if your desired currency is not listed in the **'Home'** tab $ drop-down box, you may:

1. Select the cells you would like to change the currency

2. **Right-click** and select **'Format Cells…'**:

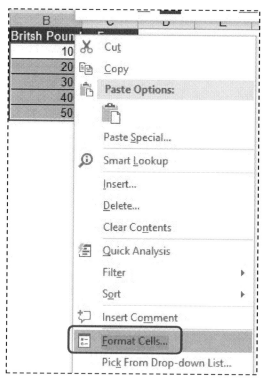

3. Select the tab **'Number'**

4. For the **'Category:'** **'Currency'**

5. In the **'Symbol'** drop-down box select your desired currency, in this example, *'£ Engilsh (United Kingom)'* was selected

6. Click the **'OK'** button

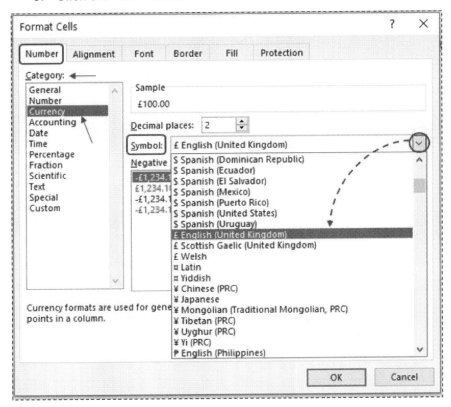

7. Repeat the preferred method above, this time for the **'Euro €'** currency

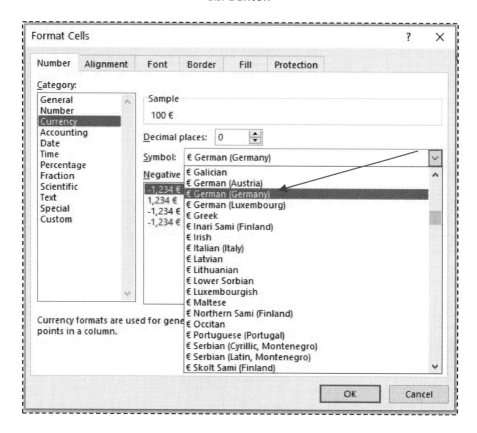

We now have currency displayed in the **British Pound £** and **Euro €**:

	A	B	C
1	US	British Pound	Euro
2	$ 100	£100	100 €
3	$ 200	£200	200 €
4	$ 300	£300	300 €
5	$ 400	£400	400 €
6	$ 500	£500	500 €

A Message From The Author

Thank you for purchasing and reading this book! Your feedback is valued and appreciated! Please take a few minutes and leave a review.

Other Books Available By This Author:

1. Microsoft® Excel® Start Here The Beginners Guide

2. The Step-By-Step Guide To The **25 Most Common** Microsoft® Excel® Formulas & Features *(version 2013)*

3. The Step-By-Step Guide To **Pivot Tables &** Introduction To **Dashboards** *(version 2013)*

4. **Excel® Pivot Tables & Introduction To Dashboards** The Step-By-Step Guide *(version 2016)*

5. The Step-By-Step Guide To The **VLOOKUP** formula in Microsoft® Excel®

6. The Microsoft® Excel® Step-By-Step Training Guide **Book Bundle**

7. **Excel® Macros & VBA For Business Users** - A Beginners Guide

8. **Microsoft® Word® Essentials** The Step-By-Step Guide

Made in the USA
San Bernardino, CA
19 June 2018